"Dad was really keen on this not being another clichéd 'rags to riches' story. But his life is the epitome of achievement. It is success that I hope shines from this book as his drive, not just wealth. In the really desperate '70s when my concerned school teacher took Mum to one side and asked if everything was OK because 'Nicholas says you have a tax man living in the loft', Dad was offered really quick (and dodgy) ways of getting money. Even though we were sitting at home with the electricity turned off he was never interested in quick fixes; for the same reason as he 'never wanted to win the pools or the lottery'.

He is about success and achievement. This motivation is perhaps what makes him so rare; it's not a characteristic that someone can choose. A great mentor and Dad, but moreover, my lifelong best mate."

Nick Dutton

100% of the authors royalties and 50% of the publishers profits from the sale of this book are being donated to charity as below:

- **The Dutton Endowment for Clinical Academic Cardiology.**
- **The Dutton Oncoplastic Research Fellowship.**

"Gary Dutton made me feel special, not because he told me so, but because of how he treated me.

It started for me in late 2005, when I sat in his office, agreeing a contract to work for him, excited to be joining the industry giant that he had built Synseal into. I felt like a footballer joining Manchester United under Sir Alex Ferguson. Over the next five years, I was to realise just how special Gary was, and got an insight into his blueprint for success.

Gary understands business models better than a Harvard graduate, but more than that, he knows the key role people play in those models. If you imagine a circuit board as a business model, Gary knows that people are the conductors that make the circuit work, and the better the conductor, the more efficient the circuit. He understands the Sellers, the Buyers and the Makers of successful products. He knows how to put 24 karat gold round pegs into round holes; choices of note include: 'Mad Dog' Malcolm Le Masurier riding shot gun, 'Dutton Jnr', with his outstanding marketing prowess, and 'The Welsh Wizard' Gareth Edwards, brought in at the perfect time, to fine tune the burgeoning Extrusion Department.

Gary's closest team will run through brick walls for him, and because he listens to them and makes them feel valued, they will do it gladly. I was privileged to feel that way, and enjoyed every minute.

Gary is a great man who has gifted thousands with prosperity and security, and continues to do so, and I am honoured to have been involved with him."

Robin Byron

Production Director – Synseal

"What you see is what you get!

A genuine down-to-earth family man with a wicked sense of humour.

From very humble beginnings, when he first started out in business many years ago, Gary has achieved immense success, which I am sure extends far beyond what he himself could ever have imagined, and deservedly so.

He has proved beyond doubt, that with common sense, a lot of hard work, dedication, perseverance and a little luck along the way, you can be successful beyond your wildest dreams.

I have nothing but the utmost respect for Gary. He is an inspiration to us all and a pleasure to work for."

Delma Jones

Gary's PA of 17 Years +

"Regardless of whether you agree with Gary's views or not, there can be no doubt this man is a winner."

Malcolm Le Masurier

Chief Executive Officer – Door Stop International

"What I have learnt, and believe covers the experience of working for Gary, and the man himself, is summed up within these anecdotes, sentiments and analogies:

"The only place where success comes before work is in a dictionary."

"Don't say we are doing our best, but to succeed in what is necessary."

"When you get a thing the way you want it, leave it alone!"

I have always personally seen Gary conducting his business as a combination of war and sport, knowing to never hold discussions with the monkey, when the organ grinder is in the room.

Straight, single minded and focused; moreover, a true, generous, and unconditional friend.

I think a fitting tribute for him in business and one of his passions (yachting) is that: the wind is only favourable, if you know to which port you are sailing".

Rob Wilkinson

Door Stop International

"I was Gary's Finance Director for about seven years, before he sold the business to an MBO, of which I am a part. His entrepreneurial capabilities must be clear to everyone who has known or heard of him, but just as impressive is his ability to select the right people to work for him, in all the different areas that are critical for success.

I found that effective decisions were made in good time, and for me, it was an encouraging environment to get things done.

He always remained fully interested in all parts of the business. Gary organised the business, so that he could concentrate on taking those few major strategic decisions, thus giving time to get them right. He is a great leader.

Work is, of course, work, but often it was simply fun. There are many stories about him; here's a couple I remember.

One of his main habits is smoking, and at the time of the introduction of the workplace smoking bans, he was horrified at the intrusion of the state into his private life. He tried to get round this by installing a bed settee and duvet in his very large office, so that it doubled as a bedroom - where, apparently, you are allowed to smoke!!

I recall one day he attempted to shoot a pigeon in his conservatory with a shotgun, missed the bird, and inevitably we sent someone round to fix the glass."

Brian Onions

Finance Director – Synseal

"I first met Gary in April 1999, when I went to Synseal to meet him and his Managing Director, Malcolm Le Masurier, and after a few hours Gary offered me the position as his Production Director.

I joined Synseal Extrusions Limited, in June 1999, which was the start of a very interesting ten years with the Company.

It was a journey that showed me the type of person he is, why he became successful, and what makes him a true entrepreneur: he is tough, knows his mind, and gets the best from his team.

Obviously, there were a lot of highs, but also some lows, and one particular event that strikes as a very difficult time, was when one of his team was sadly killed in a road accident. During this time, he showed great strength and leadership. I was fortunate to experience a part of him that only a few people get to see and know personally. He is assertive, a born leader but a very fair and generous man.

I know that I am extremely lucky to have been part of Gary Dutton's exceptional business triumphs over the past 20 years.

Gareth Edwards

Commercial Director – Synseal

"Very enjoyable read, but not as enjoyable as working with you for the last 17 years!"

Gavin Cummings BA Hons

Partner, Browne Jacobson LLP

"I first met Gary in February 2003, at my final interview for a role as Manufacturing Director (Designate). It was my first impression and insight into how Gary trusted his Board of Directors. He said 'I don't need to know if you can do the job: my guys have already done that. I just need to make sure you and I can get along'. Clearly we did and I spent the next 6 years working for Gary, very happily, learning a lot from him and, I think, teaching him a few things!

Gary's success, and the success of Synseal, is directly related to his uncanny ability to read people, and appoint the best people available into the job. You know where you stand with Gary, he makes that incandescently clear, and I would say that people who know him would always want to stand alongside him. I don't know if Gary has all the answers: what I do know is that he would always ask his Directors for their thoughts, opinions, and advice when it came to decisions that affected the business... One of his many attributes is that he makes you feel valued.

I consider it a privilege to have been part of a team of people that has contributed to his business successes, and to have been made to feel like a part of his family."

Steve Musgrave

Manufacturing Director – Synseal Extrusions Ltd

"I've only known Gary since he was successful, but three things come into mind when I think about him and the success he has had.

Firstly, his views, thoughts and philosophies on life, ranging from how to build and run successful businesses, to the problems facing the country, to the "Tarquins" in the City- I could truly sit and listen to him for hours and have had the privilege of doing do on a number of occasions.

Secondly, the way he has surrounded himself with top quality people (both within and outside the business) whose opinions and advice he trusts and listens to. Too many entrepreneurs try and do it all themselves or penny pinch on their choice of staff and advisors and ultimately pay the price. To steal from one of Gary's mantras, he truly understands the difference between value and cost.

Thirdly, that he is the boss! He may seek opinions and thoughts from others, but ultimately he makes the decision and he alone. He knows that if he gets it wrong, he is the one who will suffer but if he gets it right, he is the one who will benefit. Fortunately for all those people who have worked for him and all of the advisors like me who have benefitted from his success he has made a lot of very good decisions over the years!

Good luck with the book and here is to many more successful years ahead."

Richard Farnsworth

Tax Director, PWC

"Gary is a plain talking guy who is as comfortable chatting in the local pub as he is in the boardroom. His life story is a tale of hard work, dogged perseverance and achievement. This book distils the complex world of big business down to straightforward concepts in jargon free style. Gary explains how selling is not just an art form but also a science and provides a host of aphorisms, anecdotes and principles based on his lifetime of experience. The result is a remarkably honest and insightful perspective on the machinations of business building. Readers will be struck by the sense of satisfaction that Gary has derived from wealth-creation and the resulting freedom to support causes he believes in that this has afforded. Everyone can learn from this book - we all need skills in selling because we all at some point have something to sell. This book should be essential reading for all the would-be "Tarquins" in the city..."

Mr R Douglas Macmillan MD FRICS

I have only known Gary for 18 months, but in that short time I have got to know him well enough to convince me I should read his book, and I am glad I did. Gary has been a stunningly successful businessman and it is always rewarding to read about success and how it has been achieved. In Gary's case, it was earned rather than inherited: earned through being prepared to take risks; having the drive and conviction to see ventures through; being able to take others with him, and sheer hard work. There are important insights and messages for aspiring business leaders here. I hope the book is widely read.

Professor David Greenaway BSc M.Com D.Litt DL

Vice-Chancellor, University of Nottingham

"Gary Dutton's autobiography entitled 'Business Builder' is a must read for every aspiring entrepreneur in our country today.

His strong views, acquired through practical experience on how to 'run' a successful business enterprise are a fine example, to so many young people today.

Furthermore, he has been a past master at selecting a strong management team at all levels in his business enterprises.

I have no hesitation in recommending this Autobiography to the public at large, as it depicts, in an honest and frank manner, one man's exceptional personal achievements in life."

Sir Stanley Odell

"It shows what can be achieved by dedication, very hard work and a good wife."

Sir Harry Djanogly, CBE

GARY DUTTON MBE
AUTOBIOGRAPHY

THE BUSINESS BUILDER

Published by Amazing Authors Agency
Adventure House
91 Deanfield Road
Henley on Thames
Oxfordshire
RG9 1UU
United Kingdom

enquiry@amazingauthorsagency.com
www.amazingauthorsagency.com

A CIP Catalogue record for this book is available from the British Library.

Editor: Jonathan Blain

Assistant Editor: Bernard Dodd

Proof Reading: Linda Innes

Transcription: dictate2us

Front Cover Photograph: Norman Gent

Design: freshly-squeezed-design.co.uk

Printed in Great Britain by Lightning Source

ISBN - 978-0-9570162-0-0

DEDICATION

I dedicate this book to:

My dear mother Delphine, who sadly died during the writing of this book;

My son Nick, who is a man to be proud of;

My Dad, one of the most amiable men anyone could wish to meet;

My late beloved brother, who died thirty years before his time;

The guys past and present whose help and loyalty made the journey enjoyable and rewarding;

To my friend and colleague Malcolm who, after over thirty years with me, must qualify as a masochist;

Jonathan Blain, whose enthusiasm and help have made this book possible;

Lastly but most importantly, to my darling wife, friend and soul sister, Carol.

ACKNOWLEDGMENTS

I would like to thank everyone who has helped me in creating this book, particularly ..

Mr Jonathan Blain, the guy that motivated me to start the book, and encouraged me to finish it. His enthusiasm and knowledge have been indispensible.

Mr Norman Gent and Mr Nick Dawe for their photographic input.

Mr Antony Hepworth of Freshly-Squeezed Design .

CONTENTS

PREFACE

This is the book I have been meaning to write, or at least the book my wife said I should write. Not just rags to riches or just a business story, but with the why and the how. An emotional journey; with the ups and downs, derived convictions, philosophies and principles, views on politics, the markets, trade unions, banks, corporate advisors and society at large. I had no qualifications on leaving school, therefore had little to lose.

As a 12 year old, I had seen the bailiffs come to our council house, and heard my parents shouting at each other over money. I decided that it was never sex, politics or religion, that made the world go round, but in the main it was money; perhaps with a little love along the way.

In addition to the dedications listed, I provide the following as an indication of where I am coming from, in terms of people and things I admire:

- **John Slater for his definition of luck: 'When preparation meets opportunity'**
- **Warren Buffett for Net Jets**
- **Margaret Thatcher for her comments on the EU and society**
- **Sir John Harvey-Jones for being different**
- **Lord Norman Tebbit for his intellect and strength**
- **Enoch Powell for his vision**
- **Winston Churchill for the obvious**
- **Lennon and McCartney**
- **All the great girl singers**
- **Dr P York for pointing me in the right direction**
- **Rolex**
- **White wine**
- **The sea**
- **Mustique**

I lean very much to the right in terms of politics, mainly owing to the fact that socialism depends on its fundamental tenets of redistribution of wealth and state control. Attempting to inflict such mantras on thinking human beings is an indictment of the perpetrators' intellect and / or integrity.

If you have not thrown this book on the floor already, read on. I do hope you have a fraction of the enjoyment I gleaned from writing it. Please note some of the names which have been changed for reasons of correctness and respect.

ALWAYS BUILD ON SOUND FOUNDATIONS

INTRODUCTION... WHY?

Over the years I have been asked many times "What made you want to do what you have done in business?" Dependent on the person asking, and what I suspected their motive was, I have answered in several different fashions.

If I felt the inquisitor was being a little spiteful, and I thought they were being less than kind, I would say, "If you have to ask the question, you probably won't understand the answer."

If the question was asked for reasons of genuine interest, then I would try to reciprocate in a more helpful and sincere way. Perhaps the most honest response was that I simply wanted to prove that I could be a success at something.

I was never a great scholar, nor did I have particular athletic skills, nor a musical bent. My maths teacher once accused me of being "hopeless". Many years later in my early forties, I did manage to get a spot of revenge; I saw him in a restaurant, and although we had a very genial chat, the real buzz came when we left. By chance, his old Austin car was parked right next to my Bentley - so much for me being hopeless! My old dad used to say "there's no profit in revenge", but my goodness, it tasted sweet on that occasion.

As a small boy, I consider I was a sensitive kid, and had an upbringing where money was a rare commodity. The rows that ensued between my parents due to the lack of it, created a drive within me.

I would be disingenuous to suggest that the trappings of commercial success have not been gratefully received and enjoyed. However, I would qualify the view, by saying that my first Jaguar, bought in my early 20's, gave me far more glee than the six Bentleys, four Ferraris and a Rolls Phantom I owned as years progressed. Not complacency, I like to think, but simply the way of it. As would most people, I love all the private jet travel, the top hotels, and my yacht in the Med. More about boating later...

It's great to have money to provide extra security through private health care for my family, grandchildren at private schools, and a super home with all the gongs and bells.

Awarded an MBE, I consider myself a patriot; I would be something of a hypocrite if I wasn't. I can just about tolerate a little dishonesty IN OTHERS, but not hypocrisy. Being patriotic does not remove my right to say that money allows a degree of civility in an increasingly uncivilised world. It brings certain protections that would otherwise be unavailable. Money does not bring happiness, they often say. I agree with the sentiment, but it does give the luxury of choice. Or as a dear old friend redefined the saying, "With money you can choose your own misery."

A bit cynical, but quite clever.

In a society which often appears to want to clone citizens to the lowest common denominator rather than encourage and applaud individual endeavour, financial success is satisfying, and allows a degree of individuality that others can't enjoy.

As a child, I remember there was a cult programme on TV called The Prisoner, starring Patrick McGoohan. The theme was: "I am a name not a number." No wonder it became a cult series, and was, without doubt, prophetic.

I must say, that the £100,000,000+ which my PWC accountants tell me is my net worth, is probably not necessary to enjoy the trappings. So why did I continue? It must be that I wanted to prove to myself that I could be good at something.

From our first date, my wife of 40 years and I shared the fire and desire for wealth accumulation. The big difference was that she would have been happy to be a pools winner, or come up on the lottery. This was never for me; I craved the achievement and self-respect of doing things my way. Perhaps this was useful, since I have never done the pools or played the lottery.

I don't consider that money has changed me fundamentally; I am still the same guy I have always been. More knowledgeable of course, but not, I like to think, selfish or too full of my own importance. I do hold in awe people who have chosen other careers in, say, medicine, and I have donated large chunks of money to the causes of cardiology and oncology. I chose these causes because of the brilliant guys who sorted out my wife's illnesses some time ago.

Ok, so I was a sensitive little boy, who became driven to succeed for the reason of success itself. The trappings that go with the territory are great, but I find that most successful businessmen did not set out to be rich for the sake of being rich. In the talks that I have given over the years, I often espouse the theory that those who set out to succeed for monetary gain alone, are less likely to arrive at their Shangri-La.

As all kids do, we grow up with folks asking us what we want to do when we grow up. I used to say I wanted to be a carpenter. Or at least I did, until I got to about ten. After that, it was business building for me. Not that I had much idea how I was going to get there, I just knew I would. Not arrogance, but self-belief that if I worked hard and smart, I could do it. So can most people, if they want it enough. They call me an entrepreneur, a rather glamorous word which is often misconstrued. The closest equivalent in English is 'enterpriser', and one of my many homespun philosophies that have evolved, and which appear in my book is:

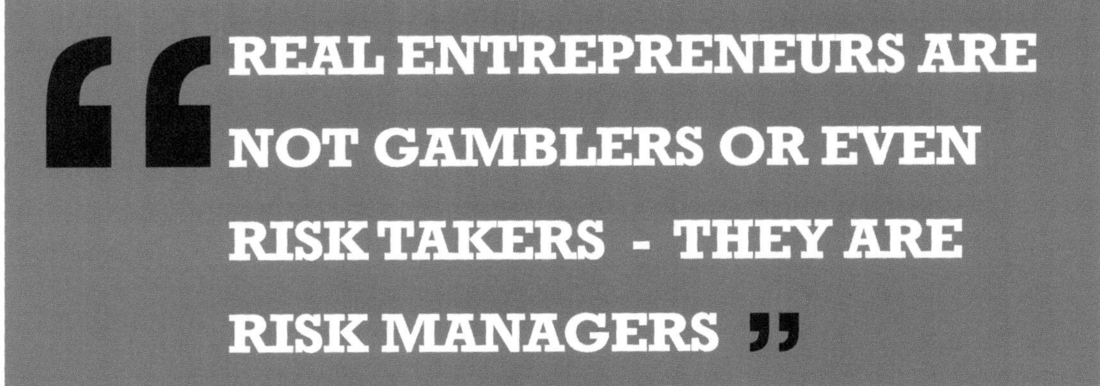

For sure, over my career, if I had been minded to put everything I had on the line, maybe I would be even more stinking wealthy than I am now. Again, when one comes from having nothing to a lot in financial terms, an inherent fear grows: of sliding back down the snake, and having to start climbing the proverbial ladder all over again. In later chapters, I describe some of the disasters and business failures, and liquidations I have experienced.

There is no substitute for failure to show you how not to do it wrong again, they say, and in part, I concur. It is also said that adversity is good for the character. My glib response is always that I have enough character, and don't need any more adversity.

Make up your own mind, but there will be ups and downs, and there is a price to pay for ambition and achievement. Some think the price is too high. I did not. •

CHILDHOOD

Me. Born March 1949, not so long after the Second World War. My late beloved brother Stewart came along three years and two months later. To begin with, mum, dad and I lived with my maternal grandparents, then after a row between my father and mum's dad, we had to move into dad's parents' house. My cot was the bottom drawer of a chest of drawers, and the house was 'home' to twenty one people. No big deal, but the house was a two and a half bedroomed semi. 'Hot bedding' is not a new phenomenon!

After a couple of years, we moved to a Nissan Hut, a corrugated sheeted, half-moon shaped place in an ex prisoner of war camp. There I had my first memories, of the stove in the middle, and the tin bath, for the obvious.

When I was three and baby bro' was just a few weeks old, the four of us arrived at our first real home: Ward Place on the Ladybrook Estate, which was a newly built council house. It was a two bedroomed place, with the only heating being a coal fire in the living room.

Granddad had performed the flitting on his old open lorry: mum, him and Stew in the cab, and dad and me on the back, with what meagre possessions we had.

SCHOOL DAYS...
GREY SHIRT

It was a very austere time, with little or no furniture, and mum and dad falling out constantly. The arguments were normally over money, or at least the lack of it. Often I had to comfort my little brother, when our parents were screaming at each other. Dad aspired to be a businessman, which was never realised; he was, however, a very personable and capable salesman. I consider that his lack of commercial achievement was due to his tendency to be a little gullible in his dealings with others. At the age of 12 and following one of father's not very successful business attempts, I remember the bailiffs coming at breakfast time. Dad, in his dressing gown, tried to reason with them. It was scary for young kids, and it made its mark on me. My parents were good people and in later years I did whatever I could to demonstrate my love and respect for them. Dad remains to this day one of the nicest people anyone could wish to meet.

I do believe that my lack of academic achievement was in part due to the fact that there was nowhere to do homework. The living room was not conducive to concentration, and the bedroom was so dreadfully cold that, like my tooth brush, the pen had ice on it in the winter. I was born left handed, which was not desirable back then, and I was perhaps a bit dyslexic, so my handwriting was, and still is, diabolical.

Things improved a little following the invention of the electric fan heater.

I remember being fearful and sensitive as a little boy, and only wanting my parents to be nice and happy, but sadly, that was rarely the prevailing atmosphere.

My father was always a nice man and has never hit me as a kid. Mother, however, was different; she would often clout me for whatever.

Mum was one of four daughters of an ex-military man, and corporal punishment was natural. To this day I don't really hold with violence, but then again, I don't like the contemporary way of no discipline. Respect is important. I fail to understand the modern attitude of trying to counsel an eighteen month old child not to put his fingers in an electric fire.

If the institution of marriage was still as it was, i.e. the bedrock of society, I believe today's degradation in society would be minimised.

The council estate was fairly rough, but with a strange sense of honour, the door was never locked, yet there were no break-ins as there are today.

Dad's mum was a lovely lady, and I found my visits to her house like an oasis of peace. Granddad Jim (dad's dad), was a dead horse and donkey dealer sort of a guy. He had a nasty temper, and taught me the sort of things that old time granddads were used to: swearing, fighting, and shooting airguns were some of my lessons from him.

Stew and I were the original latchkey kids. As the eldest, I was always responsible for sorting out the sandwich when we returned home from school. Mum always worked, as was necessary to ensure there was enough food on the table.

As I say, I was not a happy little boy most of the time, but then again I did acquire the taste for trying to improve my situation. Even as a boy, I was forever trying different things to make a bit of money. I put on film shows for the lads on the estate, sold potatoes at weekends, and made plaster models to sell to other children.

I do recall at school that I would have loved to wear a white shirt, but the grey ones stayed 'cleaner' longer; perhaps this is why I now have a very expensive wardrobe. All these things go to forming the character of a person, and I have no doubt that these hardships were instrumental in making me as driven towards success as I am.

I do believe that, unlike a lot of kids in those days, I was honest, never becoming involved with the usual petty thieving. That's not to say I was an angel, but criminality was never my thing.

In my teenage years I became a sort of Mod for a while, and that was great: the scooters, the girls, the music, the clothes, the whole nine yards. Nonetheless, my heart and head were forever focused on making money, and providing the security and elegance for which I craved.

I suppose by the time I was fourteen, I had no doubt what I was intending to do when I left school. I was to be a salesman and a businessman. I had no idea how it was to happen, I just knew that was how things were to be. Many false starts later, I realised the ambition.

Mum and Dad did their best, but with no recrimination intended, I have to say that of recent years I have come to say that:

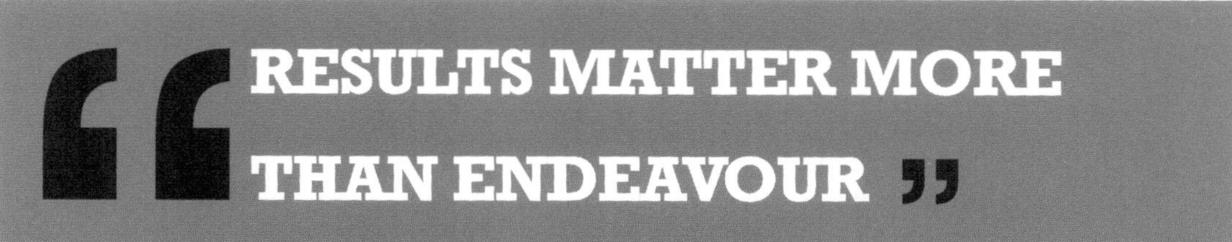

EARLY CAREER

When I left school, the careers officer asked me what I wanted to do.

I replied, "I want to build a business.

"But what do you know about building a business?" he asked, looking at me in disbelief. I told him about all the various money making schemes that I'd had as a kid."

He said, "All right then, we've got one job that will suit you."

It turned out to be as a sales assistant in a jewellery shop.

I enjoyed two parts of the work, selling the jewellery, and fixing ladies' bracelets. However, when the owner retired, the younger manager didn't like me much. He insisted that I spend my time cleaning shelves, which I hated. I was there for seven weeks before I walked out.

After that, I went to work in a stationer's. They sold quite expensive pens, and again I enjoyed the selling. I was there for about six months until one Thursday, just before lunch, I went to see Arthur, the assistant manager and told him, "I'd like a raise, please."

He frowned at me and refused. I only wanted to go from £7 per week to, say, £8. I went out for lunch annoyed, but more than that: determined.

The local paper came out on a Thursday, and there was an advert placed for Woodhouses Furniture Store. The ad was the typically non-politically correct type of advert that you wouldn't be allowed to run now, more's the pity, because they were very effective, and quite inspirational.

The advertisement read: "I'm Ken, I'm the manager of Woodhouses, which is part of GUS Furniture. I was the best salesman that they ever had in this area, and I'm looking for somebody to replace me."

As a confident young man, I couldn't pass up a chance like that. I knew I would be the best salesman, given half a chance. Over the years, I found a number of sales jobs through answering ads in newspapers.

I went to the interview and got the job, but there was only one problem. I didn't have a driving licence. The supervisor was a guy called Smith, who would have been about thirty. He was completely hopeless as a salesman, but he had an Austin Cambridge motor car. Ken, the manager, actually told Mr. Smith to drive me around in his old vehicle. With that sorted, I went back to Arthur, and told him what to do with his job.

That was on the Thursday, and I started selling furniture to householders on the following Monday. My first week's wage selling furniture was seventy five pounds, at a time when the average man's wage was £27. All of a sudden I'm thinking, "This is great!"

Direct selling always requires a premium price on the items, which is fine when you're the salesman in the days when the product is embryonic; but once the product appears in the Co-op or Comet, you're out of a job. Or at least, the potential waned significantly. This is the nature of the beast, but it didn't matter, as moving from one product to the next, never became boring. What did matter, was that every firm I worked for owed me commission when I left. It was the way that firms always tried to swindle their sales staff after they moved on.

In these very early times, I learned a lot, but perhaps most of all, I learned that there was a theory to selling. One important lesson was:

> **“THE DEFINITION OF A SALE IS THE EXCHANGE OF GOODS, SERVICES OR IDEAS MADE AT A PROFIT AND TO THE MUTUAL AND LASTING BENEFIT OF ALL PARTIES CONCERNED”**

Anything less is not selling.

From working for GUS, I moved into selling TVs for a company called Rediffusion. This business was a very big but prosaic sort of outfit. Their terms of trade made it almost impossible to produce plenty of business: they wanted a 25% deposit from people, which was very restrictive to the sales effort. There were no USPs (Unique Selling Points), and given the three basic requirements when selling anything: price, quality and service, the Rediffusion sales guys, had little upon which to build a good presentation.

At this point, it is appropriate to make mention of a crucial aspect of any professional salesman's approach to his work:

> “ ALWAYS SELL THE BENEFITS AS WELL AS THE FEATURES ”

Whilst it may seem obvious, it remains amazing how many ignore this most elementary point. An old but classic example is the Walls sausage company:

> “ SELL THE SIZZLE, NOT THE SAUSAGE ”

The one way to make good money as a salesman with Rediffusion was by selling the ‘extra radio points’. These were radio speakers installed on a wired service, which existed on many council estates at the time. Rediffusion was a household name, similar to the Gas Board or British Telecom, and as such, we could virtually knock on the door and walk in. With that control established, we just told home owners that we were there to “site” their extra points. I have put them everywhere, five or six in most houses. The householder was invariably delighted to buy these radios throughout their home, so for a while I was doing very well. Unfortunately, the company could not see the loss leader advantages available from this type of business, and after a few months changed the rules, and that was the end of that.

I quickly started work for another TV firm called Alex Owen, owned by Philips Electrical. They were supplying dual standard, 625 line, black and white televisions with BBC 2. In addition, they had a far more amenable marketing strategy. There were ten salesmen working from the branch which I joined; they were all older than me. The deal was televisions, with a slot meter on the back: an early pay-to-view system. So Alex Owen Ltd had teams of salesmen like me going out, and selling these TVs at just a £2 deposit. Now, one has to accept that marketing in its crudest form, in a free economy, is:

> **"THE SELECTION AND FULFILLMENT OF CONSUMER DESIRES IN A WAY THAT MAXIMISES THE PROFIT PER UNIT OF CAPITAL EMPLOYED IN THE ENTERPRISE"**

Which, by way of a simple analogy, means you don't travel from England to Scotland via Spain! Likewise, if you canvassed all the fancy houses, trying to sell slot TVs, the chances of getting a positive response was low. The council estate houses where they had an old Ford Cortina with no car tax on it, and stone cladding on the walls, were far better. The product and the marketing were designed for a particular market.

Two main options when creating a marketing campaign are to use spread shot, or rifle methods. There is a time and place for both, although in the main I have preferred the rifle (targeted) option.

With Alex Owen, I was earning about three times the average man's income at the age of 18. One of the added benefits was the vehicle provided for the job, a van with mattresses in the back. Laying the tellies on mattresses to keep them from being damaged was better protection than just the boxes they came in. Of course the mattresses came to have various uses – in an extracurricular fashion!

After Alex Owen Ltd, I joined Telefusion in Derby. That wasn't so nice, because not only did I have to sell their electrical goods, but the manager also wanted me to carry out repossessions. This is a fairly dehumanising occupation, because you have to be pretty robust in your approach when repossessing. You have to take the goods away there and then, regardless of the excuses people come out with, and regardless of what they say about you afterwards. Thankfully, I got out of that pretty quickly, and I briefly found myself involved in a scheme about as far removed from TVs as you could imagine: selling candy floss making machines to corner shops.

It was one of those things that should have been easy money. The concept was that we would sell candy floss making machines to corner shops for £550, from which we would receive £200 in commission. We would sell them on the basis that there was a great profit for the shop keeper: "Mr. Shopkeeper, you will be the only one in the area, and you will be making a fortune because your profit margin on candy floss is about 90%!"

The actual machine was just a converted Creda spin dryer. This enterprise ended in tears in a short time, because kids seem to buy candy floss at fairgrounds, and not from corner shops.

Following on, I had a couple of bad jobs.

Then Wally, the finance director at Alex Owen, asked me if I'd like to come back to the company I had previously sold for, in the position of general sales manager. At that point, general sales manager meant me managing three branches, with twelve salesmen in each branch. My ego was in play, but of course I was not ready. I was a good salesman, but commercially and managerially raw. I'd also missed the fact that John, the sales director, saw this as undermining him; which indeed it was.

Wally didn't rate John, and with good reason: he was very weak at his job. If I had been Wally, I'd have just fired John; but he didn't, so I was working under John, who was hostile to my appointment, to say the least. I was given the Nottingham, Leicester, and Grimsby branches. The first morning, I arrived at one of my new branches and announced that we were going to do 'blitz teaming,' where you take all your sales people to concentrate on one small area. To say the team was not really professional is an understatement. One of them had a tattoo right in the middle of his forehead.

"Ok," said I, "Can I have your attention?"

The tattoo came back with, "Fuck off!"

I knew this was not going at all well. Eventually though, I got them onside by convincing them that I was there to make them money. It didn't last long, though. John was determined to get me out, and eventually made my position totally untenable.

My next job was selling frozen food to cafeterias, and thought I was doing a good job, right up to the point where they pushed me out. It really was a question of déjà vu, after the last experience. The sell was easy-peasy, due to the fact that I was not selling a concept: the cafes had to buy from somewhere, so half my job was done before I arrived. What I hadn't thought about was that I was doing so well that it was highlighting the laziness of the rest of the sales team, and again, the sales director. I may have been a good salesman, but God, was I naive! My greatest asset over the others was that I learnt my lessons as a salesman, but most importantly I went to work - and this was a habit for which most others had long since lost the appetite.

Moving on, I sold deep freezers next, for a company called Permafacia based in Leicester. This was good for a while, but as I said earlier, when the product appears in the stores at less than half the price we were asking, the job viability is comparable with someone trying to sell buggy whips in the age of the motor car.

Next came Swiss-made food processors. The marketing concept was fantastic. Ladies' clubs around the country always want a bit of entertainment, a talk from a speaker or whatever. So the way our marketing worked was to actually get in touch with the club and ask if we could come and demonstrate our food mixers. They were great machines, so we always knew that after a good demo, the audience would buy.

Not that it was always easy, especially for a young boy demonstrating food mixers to an audience of women. One rule of this kind of presentation is that you have to very quickly 'take out' the heckler. That usually isn't a problem, though, because the heckler is often the one that the other women don't like either.

I'd do my demo, and I'd get them willing to pay the asking price, but I could have sold them for more. The fatal flaw in this, though, and one that I have tried to eradicate in my businesses over the years, is that the company was somewhat parsimonious with the salesmen's remuneration. We had to sell them for the £17.10 the company wanted, even if we could easily get twenty for them. I suggested that we should charge £20 and receive an extra one pound commission. "No!" came the reply, and I still don't quite understand why. In no way would the laws of elasticity have been deleterious to the number of units sold.

The next in this catalogue of work during my early career, was a company called Crusader Vending Machines, and it was at that point, that I attended the best sales course ever. I took myself to London and stayed at a hotel, where there were three hundred commission-only salesmen being trained five days a week for two weeks. The course was based faintly on the J. Douglas Edward's teachings. They taught closing, cashing objections, more closes, and so on. Two weeks of nothing but their system. It was brain washing, and very effective.

The brilliance of this concept was that the company's investment was based on recruiting three hundred salesmen every fortnight, and they expected that after a month there would be thirty remaining. After three months, there'd be ten of the originals left, and after six months there will be only one or two. But throughout that period, most of the recruits would invariably have sold at least one machine, because they knew someone with a factory, a launderette, a tyre service, or something, and that one sale would pay for his training. The brilliance of the strategy was, that over a period of time, Crusader built a team of some of the best salesmen possible, because they were a perfect distillation of all that filtered down.

It was then that I met my future wife I was earning really top money, and I was doing very well. I was working for Crusader, but I was also supplementing my income with another job. Again, this was a brilliant number: selling Willy Sheidegger typewriting courses. Generally, the target clients would be parents who wanted their daughter to become a secretary. Crusader was daytime work and the courses were evening work; so I did work hard and long hours, but I enjoyed the work and the rewards.

I was headhunted from Crusader by BSA Alvin, another vending machine supplier. I was recruited as Regional Sales Manager, with a team of twelve salesmen. My region was always in the top of the league. My team was well trained and well-motivated. The regional headquarters was a room in the Caesar's Hotel in Wakefield.

I had been with this company about five or six months, and was now married with a new baby. I was living in a flat, and earning around £150/£200 per week in salary and bonuses, and driving a company-supplied two litre Cortina. But then the sky fell in. I had been used to earning very good money, but always spent every penny. No money behind me, and a lot of new married man's expenditure. I was summoned to the Caesar's Hotel by Jerry, my manager.

"Yeah," he said. "I am going to have to let you go, son."

I just couldn't understand it! My team was the best performing overall, and I'd been expecting a raise or something! Jerry asked me how many of my team were really good producers.

"Three or four," I told him.

"And how many are not quite as good?"

"Maybe four or five."

Then he said, "Now, how much of your time do you spend with the bad ones, the poor ones?"

"About 50% of my time, really," I said, "Because they need bringing along."

And that was why Jerry fired me. He fired me because of one important lesson that I will never forget:

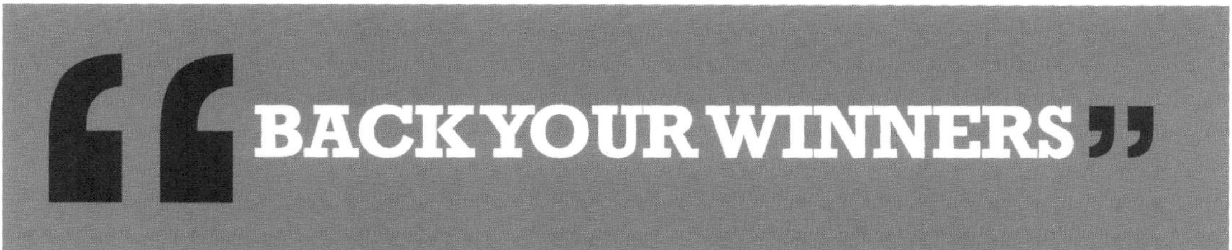

He was right, and I've learned from that, even though it left me unemployed at a time when it made things hard. Backing winners is something I've always practised since, and it has worked for me.

THE WONDERFUL WORLD OF SELLING

Ever since my days listening to my dad recite his encyclopaedia sales presentation and attending his sales masters' meeting at the age of 15, I knew that was where I needed to be, to push ahead towards the goal of being successful.

When all is said and done, everything has to be sold. Without selling there is no work for the manufacturers, the admin folks, the bean counters or anyone.

First of all let's explode a few commonly held myths:

- **Salesmen are not born. Selling is an abstract science, and although there are basic attributes which assist in the process of becoming a good salesman, there still remains a specific theory to the profession, as with many occupations. You don't expect to become a singer if you are tone deaf, you don't stand much chance of a career in medical surgery if you are blood phobic. Likewise, becoming a salesman if you had a speech impediment is difficult. Maybe an over-simplification, but it makes the point.**

- **Having the gift of the gab does not qualify a person to be regarded as a salesman. No one wants to be sold to; they actually want to make the decision to buy. That's what a professional salesman does: helps the prospect to make the intelligent decision.**

I have used the word professional twice already, and I do this deliberately. For too long, salesmanship was regarded as something of a second-rate occupation, an opinion largely procreated by wasters calling themselves salesmen. To be fair, there are good doctors and bad, good policemen and bad and there are salesmen and conmen. The two must always be divorced from each other. I will elaborate later, but in essence, conmen are fundamentally untruthful; salesmen are not.

I have many times heard the view that anyone can be a decorator, car mechanic and salesman. Clearly there is a big difference between a trained mechanic and someone who can change a spark plug. Likewise, the difference between a guy who has managed to 'sell' his old computer to his mate, and a trained professional, is enormous. In a similar vein, a representative is not necessarily a salesman. A rep can be the person who represents the company he works for, even when he goes to the post office.

Often, companies will have the sales and marketing manager or the sales and marketing director embodied within the same person. While this is not altogether wrong, it should be noted that selling is only one component of marketing; the others being advertising, promotions and public relations. I will elaborate on this later. Turning back to the salesman's world, it is often the case that the sales fraternity are regarded as something of a necessary evil by the other factions within an organisation.

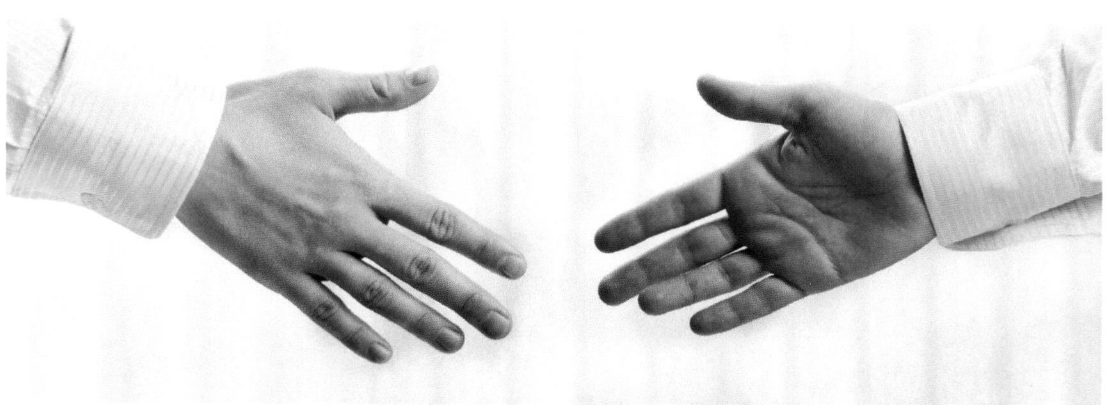

Accountants are sometimes guilty of holding such an attitude. This is due to the fact that others do not understand the job of selling, and consider that the salesman has a cushy life. Ignorance? Yes. Avoidable? Often not. But if you don't like the rules, don't join the game. Such opinions do prevail, and must simply be accepted as going with the territory.

Ok, let's now state some very straightforward questions and answers:

- **What is selling?**
  Selling is the exchange of goods, services or ideas at a profit, and to the mutual and lasting benefit of all parties concerned. Anything less than this is not selling.

- **What is the formula for success in selling?**

The formula for success in selling is 60% hard work, 25% ability and 15% planning. Of the thousands of salesmen I have employed and been associated with, I have met many who thought they were so good that they did not have to put the work in. These are generally known as 'pillocks'.

- **What are the mental steps to a sale?**

  - Involuntary attention

  - Voluntary attention

  - Interest

  - Desire

  - Action

  Obvious maybe. Irrefutable? Definitely.

- **What is the most difficult part of a salesman's job?**

Finding prospects to present to, otherwise known as canvassing. Generating enquiries is something that most people employed in the selling field dislike most. As opposed to my early years in direct selling, the marketing function nowadays often produces the 'leads' to be followed up by the sales force. Fortunately, I believe, since the old time lead-generating salesmen are increasingly a dying breed.

- **When is the best time during a presentation for the salesman to begin trying to close the deal?**

  From the moment he begins the presentation. The answers to this question are amazingly varied, but still the correct answer is "from the start"!

- **What are the most common mistakes made by salesmen?**

Not knowing when to shut his mouth. So often, a salesman will do an acceptable presentation, then ask the closing question, and then keep talking. He talks himself into a sale, and then promptly talks himself out of it. He lets the prospect off the hook. Partly this is because salesmen are of a somewhat gregarious nature, simply get carried away and don't concentrate on the theory of their work. Remember – selling is a science, an interaction between people. What would happen if an airline pilot lost concentration??

- **What is the first thing a salesman must do when commencing a presentation?**

Find out what the prospect wants and why he wants it.

Too often, salesmen fail to close the sale, because they use the art of assumption wrongly. They consider that just because their preferred colour is red, that the prospect's will be, also. Inept salesmen can be so arrogant as to decide that they know what the prospect wants and why. Big mistake! Unless you know what and why, how on earth can the presentation be centralised to engender confidence, enthusiasm and desire in a prospective buyer?

Way back in 1976, when I started one of my enterprises, The Solar Centre (yes – a bit premature in terms of timing), I had devised my presentation to amplify the features and benefits of the product. It was not difficult to achieve this, as I reckoned that there was really only one primary benefit: reducing the householder's expenditure, by providing hot water. Therefore the presentation was based on an arithmetical calculation, which produced a comparison, and a payback to the buyer in terms of savings over and above his current method of fuelling his hot water requirements. I had canvassed and obtained interest from one very nice man, who happened to be a chartered accountant.

"Great!" thinks me, "This guy will easily recognise the benefits of the savings."

I forgot my training and rules; I assumed I knew what he wanted. At the end of my presentation and several attempts at a close, he was not going along with me.

"Shit!" thought I, "Why is he not buying?"

Being a pretty highly trained and tenacious chap, I used the lost sale technique. This simply resulted in the accountant telling me that he was not truly interested in the economics of the installation. He was an ecology freak. Yes, he was concerned about the world's dwindling supplies of fossil fuels. A green, thirty years before it became fashionable.

Once this was established, the rest was simple. Present the case to give him what he wanted, and the close came easily.

Another lesson I have never forgotten.

- **What is the lost sale close?**

The lost sale close is a method used after other attempts to close the sale have failed.

Effectively the salesman asks the prospect, "Sir would you do me a small favour? I know you would benefit from buying my product, and of course it is my job to help you to do so, but before I leave, and so that I do not make the same mistake, and let down someone else who would benefit, can you tell me where I went wrong?"

When he tells you, you are right back in the fight, and can employ all the 'overcoming objection' training, and sale closing you have learnt.

- **What is direct selling?**

  Selling a one off deal, to one customer, off trade premises

  Direct selling is not as prevalent as it used to be. Many new innovations in the consumer market started their life as direct sell products. John Bloom's guys with washing machines, rental television, deep freezers, vacuum cleaners, central heating, insurance and of course double glazing, to mention but a few. Usually these products had a short life expectancy as direct sell products, owing to the fact that after a year or so, the stores caught up, and the product had lost its mystique. The prices of the product reduced with the passing of time. Nevertheless, the introduction of major innovations had their roots as direct selling products, whereby the top sales guys made a lot of money selling the benefits of a new product. Quite often, the presentation included a strong element of appealing to the part of human nature whereby people want to be seen as clever and adventurous, in being the first to buy this new invention.

- **What is a don't?**

The belief that hungry salesmen are good salesmen is daft. Anxiety is contagious, and when the guy presenting is desperate, he will transmit this anxiety. As such his competence will be significantly impaired.

- **More don'ts!**

  Don't use 'bad' words. Don't ask someone to 'sign' an order. They may be prepared to 'OK it' but don't like the idea of signing.

  Don't say 'sell', say 'buy'.

- **Classic mind set of professional successful salespeople:**
  1. When you have done your 'last' call of the day, do another one.
  2. Go selling with another guy occasionally. It will lift the morale, alleviate some of the loneliness, provide a sounding board, and a mirror for any bad habits that might have evolved.
  3. Try to develop the art of the negative close. This is a classic piece of human psychology. If you say to someone, "Do you want this straight away?" they will often react that they don't. If the same person is told, "You know, this is not available to you now," they may well respond that they want it sooner rather than later.

4. A good salesman can swap products with little difficulty. The same basic theory applies to selling a car as to a house, an ornament, or a study course.
5. It is essential to have enthusiasm in order to convey enthusiasm.
6. Plan your work and work your plan.
7. There are only two fundamental motivators: the greed of gain, and the fear of loss. The pro's invariably favour the latter. The all-time great insurance salesmen were exponents of the fear of loss presentation.
8. Learn how to ask for the order.

You may by now have realised that I am, and always was, passionate about selling. It is exciting, satisfying and can make heaps of cash for the top guys in their field. I am not as good as I used to be. A bit like older snooker players, it's not exactly a physical occupation, but after certain age there is deterioration in concentration, and the same applies to sales people.

Of all the salesmen in my life, the best four in my era were: Tony, Tim, George and me. The order of merit varies according to which of the four of us you speak to. George worked for me in the Synseal retail days. Tim is still with Synseal, and spent 15 years with me when I owned the business. Tony is one of the few top sales guys who turned out to be a very successful businessman in later years. I worked with him selling food mixers to ladies clubs; he worked for me selling showers, and I did for him, selling deep freezers... Halcyon days.

I could go on forever with sales anecdotes, theory, experiences, and general knowledge. For those who are interested in developing a career in selling, there are many books, CDs, etc. that give training and education. Suffice to say that there is one trainer who has been often copied but never bettered, in my opinion. His records have been around since vinyl long player days, and are now in CD format. Forty years ago, as a teenage salesman I would sit and listen, rehearse and memorise the tactics he described before going out to do my job. I know they have earned me very considerable amounts of money over the years. The author is J Douglas Edwards. Three of his records are called *Thirteen Closes of Sale*, *More Closes* and *Cashing Objections*. The total of about 6 hours of tuition does not sound a lot; but believe me, anyone who listens, learns, assimilates and above all uses the information and education provided on these recordings will immediately promote himself to the ranks of the top 30% of salesmen, no matter what he is selling.

If more evidence were needed, let's take the *Thirteen Closes of Sale*. Most salesmen know five, and use three. There lay the difference between the pro's and the peons.

One additional point of caution for sales people... the Rainbow Trap. In my early career and working within a team of guys there was a situation where I sold an average of one point seven machines each week. This provided me with a very substantial income on a regular basis. I will never forget another one of the team attending the weekly sale meetings who reported that he was seeking to secure a deal for 40 machines with a large and well known organization. Owing to the ineptitude of the sales manager (who could not sell water to a dying man in the desert) this chap was encouraged to pursue this activity. The lesson here is that, firstly the more call backs you do there is a proportionate reduction in the percentage chance of ever sealing the deal. The second problem when selling on a commission only arrangement is that there is no income for the duration and that eventually creates a situation where the salesman has passed the point of no return. Sayings like "bird in the hand" and "chasing rainbows" come to mind. •

YOUNG MAN, MARRIED AND WITH PROBLEMS

By now, you may have noticed that my book hopes to tell a story of a fellow from a fairly modest background, who set out to prove that he was capable of achieving something. More important to me, is the opportunity to tell my own story as a backdrop for an advisory document for people such as I used to be. Just possibly, some 20 year old Gary will find one or two areas of identification, and be able to use some of the anecdotes and advice contained within this offering. I set out to write a 'dos and don'ts, how and why' book.

Just to rewind, for a year up to being married to Carol, with baby Nicholas, the early selling years were exciting times, but had very low moments also. I had earned tons of money on occasions, and spent every penny, being a young fellow doing what young fellows do. Unlike most guys at the age of 18-20, I had not continued to run with the same set of people my age. I was earning more money, wearing good suits, driving a sports car, going out with nice girls, and going about with older men. I always found these older guys more interesting. In the selling business, the players were invariably characters, and had something to impart. Perhaps not unsurprisingly, as time has moved on, there has been something of a role reversal. A lot of the people I know nowadays are my son's age, and I think they enjoy some of my anecdotes and homespun philosophies, just as I did years ago, listening to others.

My time with gambling was a salutary lesson. Being a young man in an older men's world had its dangers. I had the cash and frequented the clubs and became temporarily hooked. It is not possible to get the buzz from gambling unless you play for more than you can afford to lose. The cure was swift, when I lost all my cash at the casino, and then stupidly lost all the deposits I'd collected from customers, that I needed to pay into the company I was working for at the time. The result was borrowing money from a loan shark, and having to work for six weeks to pay it back at crazy interest.

All the time, I was looking for the chance to move ahead in the business world. One enterprise that departed from the selling work, involved a good friend. Terry, who was five years older than me. When discotheques were not really what they are today, we rented a room above a pub in Lincoln, and with some basic sound equipment, we opened a disco club. It was a great success, and we earned well for about a year, before the fire officer limited our room to 111 people. As we were used to 400/500 customers, the viability died a death. All the same, good fun, good money, and then there were the girls, who always liked us disc jockeys. I was living the high life most of the time.

After our own disco, Terry and I would perform our disco show for people like Peter Stringfellow at the Mojo club in Sheffield, or the Dungeon club in Nottingham for Mick Parker. Often these gigs were all-nighters on Saturday. There are two pitfalls I would want to warn against. Firstly, burning the candle at three ends takes its toll on health. I became very tired and wound up having a couple of weeks in bed at the age of 18, due to being exhausted. The other problem I experienced was losing a bit of reality. I suppose many teenagers struggle to 'find themselves', but with me it was exacerbated by the lifestyle. I started to believe what some of my older friends were saying about me, that I was a brill salesman; a guy going places, etc. Maybe they were correct, and maybe they were not; nevertheless it went to my head, and for a while I lived in what I call a dark place.

"WHEN I WAS 20, I WAS MINDED TO BELIEVE I WAS A GENIUS. WHEN I GOT TO 35, I WAS NOT SO SURE. WHEN I GOT TO 50, I REALISED THAT IN MANY WAYS, I WAS JUST AN AMBITIOUS AND NAIVE LAD AT 20"

Carol was a very beautiful girl, a year older than me. She came from a similar background, and grew up some five miles from Ladybrook Estate where I lived.

We knew each other by name, but had lived different lives as teenagers. Carol had broken free, and was living in a lovely flat in London, owned by a friend of hers, Julie Grant. Julie was a well known pop singer at the time. Carol's crowd were the stars of the day: The Moody Blues (of Nights in White Satin fame), The Hollies (He Aint Heavy), and many others. Meantime, I was mixing with my older and more commercial pals, and living the life of a would-be playboy. Carol was fascinated by me being a salesman, not having really known such a creature, previously. One big thing we had in common was the fire for success, and all that went with it.

I invited Carol to a party, which an old girlfriend of mine had rather naughtily asked me to attend. Naughty, because it was her engagement party, and she had a plan that she could marry this guy from a well-off family, and still continue the dalliance with me. I asked Carol because she was great-looking and stylish, and would eclipse all the other girls at the party, including my ex. The rest is history, as they say. We met in the November, married in the July, and Nick was born the following February.

Carol's dad, Charles Hilton Riley, an ex-tank commander in WW 2, was not best pleased when he discovered that his beautiful only daughter was pregnant. He did threaten to shoot me with his old army Smith and Wesson revolver, and me being a cocky and sometimes fairly daft chap, I said something like

ME AND THE NEW MISSUS

"Who's going to marry your daughter if you shoot me?"

Anyway, after Nick was born, Father-in-Law and I became good friends, since he was delighted that I had sired a son. Mother-in-Law Dorothy was always, and has continued to be, an avid supporter of her son-in-law.

This brings us back to where I left the story at the end of the last chapter. Within a period of not much more than 18 months, from living our respective lives that many would envy, we were married with child, no money saved, no-one with money to help us, living in a tiny flat over a shop and I was out of work. The same as when I was born, there was little or no furniture apart from Carol's old bed and wardrobe, which we pretentiously called a bedroom suite. I mean, no carpets, no nothing. Clearly, if Carol had not have been pregnant, we would have planned our marriage, and acquired the necessary accoutrements to create at least a basic living situation. Being born out of wedlock may seem somewhat anachronistic now, but then it was pretty much frowned on.

After our two days' honeymoon in Scarborough, we moved into the flat using my old grandad's lorry. Oh! Déjà vu! The first morning, I borrowed spoons from the kind shopkeeper below; eating cereal without spoons is not easy. The electricity was turned off for weeks, because I did not have the £26 to pay the bill. It was not pleasant, living by candlelight. Making the baby's milk feed had to be performed using the gas stove in the flat. It was such a massive culture shock for both Carol and I, it is difficult to describe. Without the slightest reflection on my wife, I can honestly say that I do resent having married so young. It was a truly torrid time.

Having been fired from BSA Alvin for not backing winners, I spent a lot of time in the phone box outside the flat applying for selling jobs. That brings me to another conviction I have come to believe along the way:

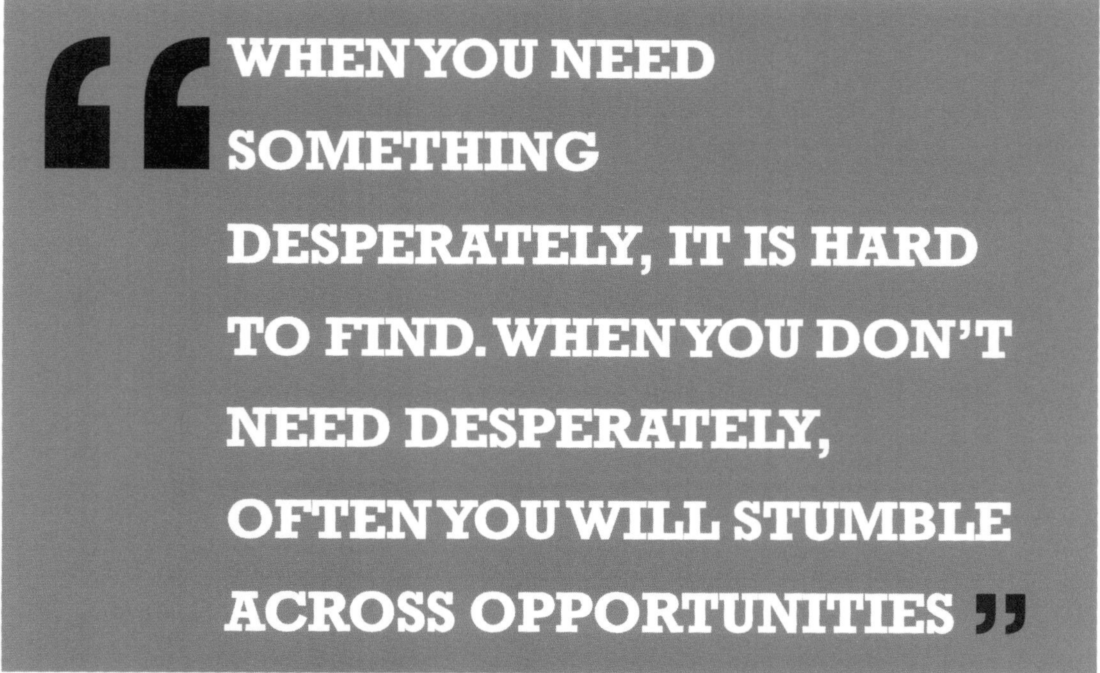

I believe this applies through life in general.

The six weeks I spent on National Assistance were humiliating, but I had to feed the family and pay the rent. There was no other way. Until then, there were selling jobs aplenty, but all of a sudden they dried up, or maybe I had lost my edge for a while.

The real sickener was walking down to the Black Bull pub for a pint one evening at 10.15pm. I could only afford one pint, so had to go late, with two shillings and four pence in my pocket. This was the price of a pint of beer then. The landlord told me that ale had gone up to two shillings and six pence. I could only afford half a pint, and that hurt badly. At the same pub one night I met up with one of my older friends called Gordon; he would be sixty then, and me, twenty. In the past, Gordon had run a chip shop, and for a little time my friend Terry and I had a deal with Gordon, where we bought fresh cut chips from him, and delivered them to the local factory canteens each day. The canteens always preferred fresh to frozen.

Gordon told me of a guy who had a juke box and pin-table business, based in Newark, and he was looking for a good salesman. Off I went, got the job and a little mini estate car thrown in. That was the start of the turnaround.

Next, I come to my wife calling me an angry young man.
I prefer a 'driven young man'. •

ANGRY YOUNG MAN OR JUST AMBITIOUS

Ok, so we now have an income, and I am back on the selling scene, working for Alberken, selling to pubs, clubs and the like.

The time on National Assistance was certainly one to focus the mind. They say that adversity is good for the character. Maybe so, but following loads more adversity, I have often since stated that I have as much character as I want, and don't need any more adversity. In reality, of course, it just goes with the territory: the more you want to achieve, the higher the chance of encountering adversity and setbacks. This applies in direct proportion to two things: firstly the magnitude of the ambitions, and secondly the degree of preparation the individual has received. In my case, I had no formal business training, and a mountain of ambition, so there were always going to be shedloads of grief along the way.

Looking back at the National Assistance experiences, had they not been so devastatingly horrible, humiliating and degrading, they could have been viewed as almost funny. The tubular steel chairs were fixed to the floor so that the 'applicants' could not throw them at the staff, I was told. There was the woman who rushed in, dumped three young kids on the counter, and screamed at the staff, "You keep the bastards!" The guy who had collected his donation in the morning, then got pissed and called back for another hand-out in the afternoon was interesting, too. What was a little more worrying, was that he actually received more cash. There can be no more enlightening insight into the world of social help, than the NAB offices back then.

I am selling the juke boxes, married with a baby, and living in the rented flat. The selling hours were more or less the times when pubs and clubs were open. This meant the middle of the day and evenings. By now, I was as good a salesman as anyone in the game, but I was a completely nondescript businessman. I later became a better salesman when I acknowledged that the really top sellers were also capable businessmen. All the same, I was 20 years old, and had studied the art and science of selling, and did well with the juke boxes for a year to eighteen months. Not only was I able to provide an income for my family, but almost as importantly, was the mini estate car which Alberken provided with the job. This transport was not what I had been used to as a junior playboy only a couple of short years ago, but then I had no choice but to focus on the reality of my present position, and as my old grandad used to say, "A second class drive is better than a first class walk."

Three things were made possible with transport: doing two more jobs, and being able to visit Mansfield reference library on Saturday mornings to further my commercial education.

During Carol's pregnancy she had accompanied me selling the typewriting courses for Willy Sheidegger Ltd. Naturally, Carol remained in the car, but I do admit to using her a couple of times, when I needed a sympathy shove with a difficult prospect. By that, I mean that I would ask if I could bring my pregnant wife into the client's house, so she could keep warm. It worked like a dream, the client would naturally accede, and then we were all friends. I don't recall having ever failed to close a deal when I used this ploy.

The concept of the typewriting course was again quite brilliant. I mentioned earlier, the food mixers to the ladies clubs. Now, Willy Sheidegger was equally well thought out. The market for the product, which was actually a service, was targeted at young girls with mediocre education, usually from working class backgrounds. The parents often wanted the girls to stay out of the factories when they left school, and the best option was seen as secretarial work. The cleverness came from the fact that we were not actually selling the course in the truest sense, we were interviewing the girl, and virtually ascertaining from the parents that they thought their kid was brainy enough to learn to type. Can you imagine a parent thinking their little Sharron was too thick to type?

The other two great parts of this job were the fact that we actually left a typewriter with the girl at the point of sale: wonderful for making the close, and for extracting the £3 deposit there and then. The second good part, was that the £3 deposit was also the salesman's commission. I could go to work with no petrol money to get home, sell half a dozen courses, fill the tank and get a drink and a cigar on the way home at 9 or 10 o'clock. Just a comment on the finances I refer to. Bearing in mind that we are going back some 40 years, if one uses the very rough and ready calculation that money loses half its value every decade, then a £45 course then, would be, say, £700 today, and the deposit some £50.

Following an enforced break, due to having no vehicle, I was now reunited with transport courtesy of Alberken and back to selling typewriting courses along with my 'proper' job selling juke boxes. That's two jobs. But then, in addition, another older friend, Reg, told me that his cousin needed someone to stand markets occasionally. Never one to miss an opportunity, off I went filling the mini estate car full of sweets and chocolates, and setting up the stall on local open markets. My pay was 20% of the takings, and this, along with the other work, proved to be enough to get my little family and me back on the straight and narrow, at least to the point where we could pay the bills.

As ever, I was looking to improve the situation and get where I knew I aspired to be. I began reading reference books at the library, and getting the basics of company formation, administration, laws, structures etc. What a wonderful thing the internet has become, for such studies!

Perhaps I was a bit of an angry young man, but I still prefer to think I was ambitious and driven. Driven by not only the desire to succeed and prove I was good at something, but moreover, to ensure that the misery and indignity of poverty did not return. As things progressed, there would be many more setbacks. Some may say I am obstinate. Naturally, I would prefer the description 'tenacious'.

By way of describing more motivational events I experienced, the first Christmas as a married man with a child was pretty horrendous. Nicholas was coming to his first birthday, and it was prior to the renaissance described above, when I got back on my feet. I recall having bought my baby a cheap teddy bear as his present. I remembered the days only three years earlier when I would be partying with the 'in-crowd' at this time of year, but that seemed like light years ago.

The frustration and fear had exploded on Christmas Eve when I met a friend who offered to buy me a drink at the Reindeer pub. In the gents' toilet I became overcome and silly. With tears in my eyes, I punched a hole in the loo door; very childish, but I hope understandable. For the record I have been able to treat Nick to more than a teddy bear over the years that ensued.

By the second Christmas, things were better, and then came the only time I can honestly recall anyone giving me anything. Carol's maternal grandma was the most delightful and kind person, as was her husband Albert. Grandma Evelyn had, for some Godforsaken reason, always liked me, and had been a great supporter and, even, my fan. She would say, "That lad's going places, you mark my words!"

To explain, they were living in a council bungalow, and had never had anything more than a few hundred pounds, but they decided to give us £250 deposit to buy a little bungalow, newly built in Mansfield. There were two types of bungalow in this thirteen property development. Some were £4,450 and the others £4,150. It may seem unbelievable now, but the mortgage on the dearer property was not possible, so the lesser priced one became our home for the next 12 years.

There had been a property called Pear Tree Cottage that both Carol and I would have given our eye teeth for, but at £6,950, it might as well have been £6,950,000. When I drive past Pear Tree now, it gives me mixed feelings of comfort and melancholy. It would probably fetch half a million at today's prices, but I could afford £5 million if I wanted it. All the same, the joy of having it back then would have been totally overwhelming. Anyway, bless Grandma Evelyn. Many

CAROL, ME, LITTLE NICK AND FIRST BORN (GRANDDAUGHTER EVE) AT THE PALACE

years later, my son Nicholas named his first daughter Eve. He too loved his great Grandma.

Around the early seventies, the laws changed concerning gambling, and the owner of the pin table company decide to downsize his operation. Clearly, the services of an effective salesman became surplus to requirements. In any event, I was looking for the next move up the ladder. Willy Sheidegger pulled out of the UK, and the market stall job was always somewhat hit and miss. It was time to move on.

I did have a look at three other positions that were advertised. One of these was a pet food company, another a meat slicing machine company, and the third a company specialising in the sale and installation of Wrigley's chewing gum machines. The first two were non-starters, the companies were very old hat and they would never have understood the dynamics of a modern sales regime. Their products were not suited to a direct sale methodology, and really they were looking for people who wanted to spend the next thirty years climbing the slippery corporate pole, to arrive at some fairly mediocre position in the organisation. Clearly these were not for me. I did indeed give the chewing gum firm a go, but again, they needed merchandising reps, not salesmen and as such, the earning potential was very limited. The chewing gum job lasted a matter of weeks only. I had about 20 different jobs, agencies, ventures and occupations in the 7 years since leaving school. Many of these ran concurrently, such was the life of a guy in my chosen profession.

My old mate Reg came into play again, telling me of a company with branches in Nottingham, Ashton-under-Lyne and Leeds: Beauty Lyne Bath Co. In truth, the word 'branches' was a little grandiose, since they were cheap rented offices. Nevertheless, I knew of this outfit, and was enthused to join them. Just as an aside, Reg was older than my dad, and was a real character. When he passed away in 2006 at 85 years of age, he was in The Canary Islands diving into a swimming pool along with two Sri Lankan girls and had a heart attack.

Having been interviewed by Brian Whyte and Tony Diston for the manager's job at Beauty Lyne, I started straight away. The staff at my Nottingham branch consisted of Joan, the middle-aged, overpaid and fairly miserable book keeper; Ann, the sexy seventeen year old clerk, and Jim, the only salesman. He was a pleasant guy but did not have a clue about selling. The business involved the sale of bathrooms, showers and wooden windows, which were then installed by subcontractor tradesmen. Over the next couple of years, I enjoyed building my first real infrastructure of salesmen from scratch. My team were: Colin in Nottingham, Maurice in Derby, Keith in Doncaster, Tony in Sheffield, then Geoff and Ray, who became friends of mine. We did well, although I was working from 8.30am sorting the installations, and then going out selling in the evening, often accompanying one of the sales guys. The day usually finished about 30 miles from home at 9.30/10 pm. The norm was to have a drink at a pub and go over the night's achievements.

The owner of Beauty Lyne was a pseudo Anglo-American guy called Ernie. He was sharp, but no commercial genius, and he lived very well out of the company. I recall one momentous occasion, when we were hammered on the Manchester TV news for some scurrilous techniques one of the sales guys had perpetrated. As we all sat thinking the end of our world was nigh, in came Sid, another great character. He decided to turn adversity into a benefit. He advertised our service and products in the usual way through the newspapers, only this time he put a big flash across the ads stating: "As Seen On TV." The lead input nearly doubled. Who said there's no such thing as bad publicity?

Brian Whyte was the company secretary and had received some formal finance control training. He and I became friends, and we discussed the fact that Beauty Lyne would not survive much longer. Both ambitious young family men, we set about planning our own venture. This was to be a copy of the business model of Beauty Lyne, but we, of course, would do it better.

The two of us rented a cheap office in Nottingham, one in Manchester, and one in Leeds. We had secured the services of the Beauty Lyne branch managers, along with the field sales staff and contractors.

Inevitably Beauty Lyne went bust, but we were ready to rock and roll. Pendale Construction Ltd was born. It was exciting and we thought we would be millionaires in short order.

Just before I continue with the story, there are a few very important points to make at this juncture: advice which I commend to anyone who wants to listen:

> **“NEVER START A BUSINESS WITH SOMEONE WITH THE SAME SKILLSET AS YOURSELF”**

All this does is duplicate effort, and produce a viability drain at the worst time in a small business's evolution.

> **“THE ONLY BAD SHIP IS A PARTNERSHIP”**

My experience tells me that partnerships are great for tennis and bridge, but in business, they struggle to stand the test of time, and will invariably prove to constrain the development of the business. At best, you are so polite to each other that, in effect, it is taking two people to make the decisions that one could easily make. In a worst case scenario, when things are not going too well, the partners begin to blame each other for the lack of progress. Whether this is actually true or not is irrelevant; it murders the business. For the record, and where the partners are men, I have often witnessed wives become prime movers in the mutual antagonism that grows between the husbands. Never try to compete with pillow talk; you will lose. One wife thinks her man is doing more than the other, and the other wife considers that her guy is better than his partner, and invariably the whole venture spirals downwards.

Now, it is appropriate to state my first rule for success in business. If I never tell anyone anything about business building again, I believe with my heart and soul that this is the big one.

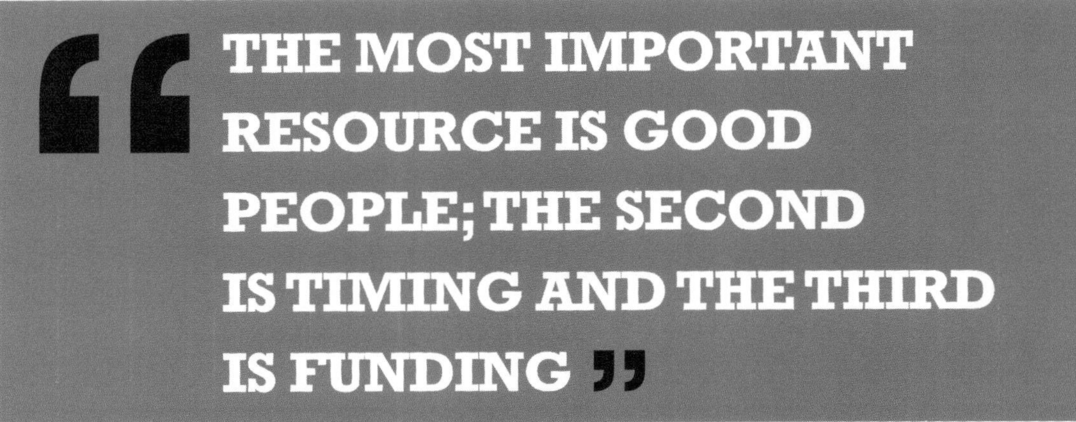

Before I return to my story, the matter of shared equity between the management personnel of a company is worthy of mention. Even if the equity is not in equal parts, there remains a strong possibility of stakeholders with small stakes becoming infected with "Proprietorial

Syndrome". Basically there grows an increasing attitude, which is personal and political, and is damaging to the wellbeing of the business. Don't misunderstand, good people are the very backbone of any company, and you must pay for the best, but try to steer clear of creating a political rod for the future. I know some are diametrically opposed to my view in this regard, but it has stood me in good stead. To quote a maritime metaphor, there can only be one captain of a ship. Always listen to your people's opinions and ideas, but when the decision has to be made, there can only be one boss. Be a benevolent dictator, or a dictatorial democrat, but always be aware of the political bullshit that destroys many good firms.

Back to my story. There we are, Brian and me, equal partners of our three office empire, heading for the sky. Him the bean counter, and me the sales guy. A while down the road, and we start to see cracks appearing in the business: our ability and our relationship one with the other. Somewhat cleverly, we did recognise the problem before it was too late. We agreed on a strategy to sell the Leeds branch to the guy we had running it, for £1000, and Brian would take total ownership of Manchester, and, of me, Nottingham. The guy in Leeds had a fairly well-off family and he had no problem paying us the grand. Brian, as I recall, bought a small Hockney painting with his £500, and me an old sports car, which was a complete waste of money.

Now on my own, with my destiny in my hands alone, I buy a new car, a Jaguar XJ. Pretty stupid, but I loved it so much. It was a demonstrator with red leather upholstery, and by God, I was sick in early 1976 when I had to sell it quickly to raise some cash. •

ONWARDS AND UPWARDS BUT SOME DOWNWARDS

From my two-roomed office on Clarendon Street Nottingham, I ran my business called Pendale Construction Ltd. Not really a construction business in the accepted sense, but it gave certain credibility to what was essentially a bathroom and shower sell and fit operation.

I had little or no idea at this stage about budgeting, cash flows or any of the basics of a proper business. There was Pat, my secretary; the rent of £6 per month (yes, £6 per month), and a bunch of subcontractors. There was Paul the plumber, Roy and Ady the joiners, Ron the brickie, and Brian the apprentice. Pete Oakley, an electrician, became a dear friend after he worked for me in these early days. Ray Britton and Geoff Goring were amongst my team of salesmen at this time. We again became close mates for several years. I met Ray when I decided it was time to branch out.

I had the services of the lads who were tradesmen, and I had identified the opportunity to buy terraced houses that needed upgrading. The twist to this, and the earner, was the council improvement grant system. I would buy an old house that often had no inside toilet or bathroom, apply for a grant to improve it, send the men to carry out the work and then sell it on. In the `70s the average price for this type of property was about £1500. The grant would be, say, £1000, and the cost of the work approximately the same as the grant. The sums were easy enough: net cost after grant, £1500; sale value £2500; therefore a grand a time profit. The first of the 22 I bought and sold was 36 Charles Street, Mansfield Woodhouse. I chose to sell it though Alan Vine Estate Agents. The manager at the branch was one Ray Britton. I instructed him to sell the house on the Thursday at 9.30am, and he called me the same day to say it had sold. Wow, what a result! Ray left his job at Vine's Estate Agents, and joined me as a salesman. Alan Vine proved to be the catalyst for my Pendale business going bust some time later.

Onwards and upwards. Pendale was doing OK, and my property refurb venture was putting some jam on the cake. Oh dear, I started to think the balloon would never burst. How wrong I was. Carol and I, living in the small bungalow on Windsor Gardens, Nick now a lovely little boy, and we were starting to have a social life. We were partying and having a bit of fun. After a while and having made a few thousand pounds from the property deals, I committed perhaps some classic, but nonetheless stupid, mistakes. At the age of 24, I go and buy a new Jaguar XJ6. I was so thrilled with the car, but goodness knows, I could have spent the money far more wisely.

Next big mistake, I recall saying to Carol when driving in my beautiful car, "I think Pendale can be run by Pat my secretary". No reflection on Pat, but that was about the daftest thing I could have come out with.

Naturally, I was looking to expand my business activities, and set up Regency Coachworks Ltd. This was a small motor body repair business. I had a guy called Ivor, another example of my philosophy of finding a 'man that can' working with me on the technical side. Although he was good at this job, he did not show up on time, and things started to go downhill. Ivor and I had a blazing row, culminating with him leaving in a fairly acrimonious manner. That meant Regency Coachworks was no more; my first company liquidation, in the summer of 1975.

It was around this time that I met David, a newly qualified chartered accountant, who occupied an office above mine on Clarendon Street. David and I were to remain involved for some 18 years. Following the failure of my motor body repair venture, it became clear that I had neglected Pendale Construction quite badly. Talk about the bird in the hand theory: this was classic evidence and formed another long held principle. In later years, when I came across a proposition that appealed to my commercial streak because it was different and colourful, my discipline was:

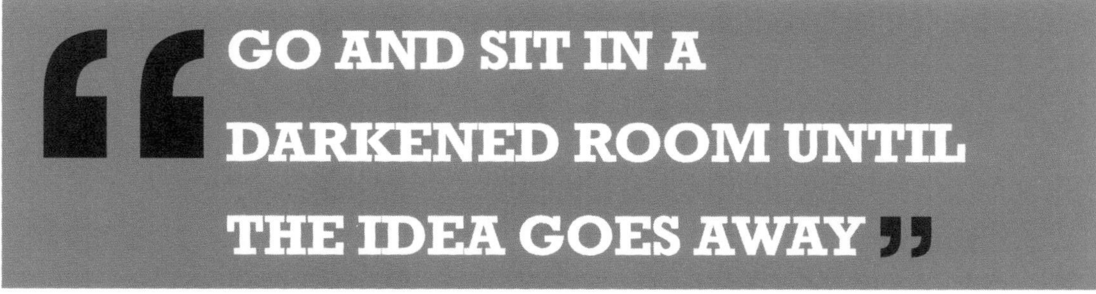

I firmly believe that without having developed this ethos, my later success with Synseal would have been impaired or non-existent.

As the saying goes, as one door closes, another slams in your face. Pretty bad times ensued. My parents became divorced in a very messy fashion: Mum was totally distraught when Dad left for another woman. Carol and I were constantly arguing and falling out, and living beyond our means. I lost my driving licence for speeding and then I stood for the most blatant three card trick at the hands of the aforementioned Alan Vine, the estate agent. I have used the lesson I learned from this man in years since.

As well as his estate agent company, he also had a number of residential properties which he let out. His M.O. was to call me and ask for my little Pendale Company to fit bathrooms and showers in these old houses. He would be the epitome of charm, asking after my wife and little boy, and then paying me up front. Having yet to learn the finer points of cash flow, this was like all my birthdays coming together at once. This conditioning took place several times, and then came the sting. Vine lived in a very nice house in an upmarket part of Nottingham. He invited me to do work there, and I built a bedroom and double garage with all the trimmings. There was a sauna and all manner of fancy fittings. The previous method of paying me in advance now ceased, to the extent that I did not even receive the stage payments which we had agreed. The upshot was him acting in a completely contrary fashion to his former way. Instead of being charming and ultra-pleasant he would call me, screaming and swearing, and generally being an archetypal bully. This was his way of keeping me off balance, and as I say, it is a method that I have adopted a few times since. Not, I hasten to add, to rip off people,. I sometimes use the old saying:

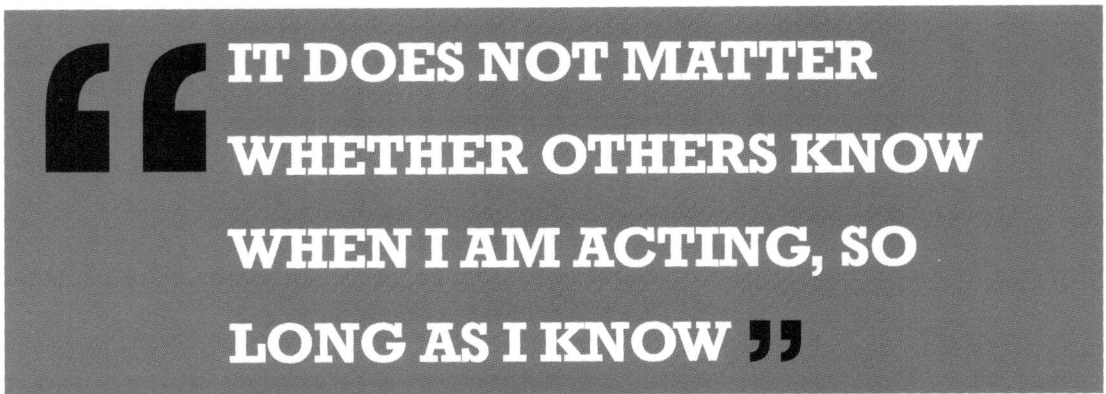

I believe it was General Patten that coined the phrase.

The end was now fairly inevitable. I did not get my money and could not get around for work, owing to not having a driving licence. Then, the Inland Revenue came for their tax, for which I hadn't the cash.

On January 16th 1976, David (my new accountant friend) suggested I went to see Roger, the insolvency expert at a local firm of accountants, for advice. This was an experience, but not one of the more pleasant varieties. I was naïve, and told Roger that I was intending to try to pay off some of the creditors. He told me not to be so stupid, and to go and get £1000 for his fee, after which he would wind up the company.

I was not proud of myself, but recalled the miserable times when dad did the 'honourable thing' which caused so much deprivation to my family, when my brother and I were growing up. In any event, my aspirations to do the right thing were silly, as I had no chance of raising any money. The only way to get Roger's £1000 was to sell the Jag. Of course, when selling in a hurry the price is at rock bottom, but it had to go. The creditors' voluntary liquidation process was under way and the fallout was horrible. I had managed to retrieve an old Transit van from the assets of Pendale, and this was now my mode of transportation, something quite demoralising after my Jaguar. Being naive and thinking people would understand, if not sympathise, I visited three creditors, and although one older guy, Arthur Baker, was very decent with me, the others were far from understanding. One took a swing at me, and the others were seriously obnoxious.

Now back at an all-time low, I had to look to making a living, and generate an income. With the blessing of having my licence back and the luxury of the old Transit, I had little choice but to try to set up again.

Using a similar concept to Pendale, David, my accountant, formed Edenstone Builders Limited for me. I retained the services of some of the contractors from the past and with a few pounds left over from selling the car, I spent the next several weeks working night and day to get some work in the old bathroom and shower market.

There were some tangential problems, one of which was a visitation by some creditors to the office on Clarendon Street. As you might imagine, their purpose was not to enquire after my wellbeing. The answer to this was to swap offices with David. He had an office on the second floor and mine was on the first. The simple act of swapping meant that any callers looking for me went to his 'new' office and not upstairs to where I was now situated.

Just as I thought things could not get much worse, of course Sods' Law kicked in. While labouring on a house I had sold, I bust my ankle. Oh shit. It was my left ankle, which meant no manual vehicle, and guess what? The old van was manual. I hired a small automatic car, which I could not afford, and when driving home from Nottingham to Mansfield one night a week later, I had a car run into the side of me and turn the hire car on its roof. So there we are: mid-winter, skint, ankle knackered, somewhat humiliated, and generally fed up, but at least making a living, and still seeking the opportunity to make my fortune.

I mentioned earlier the older, good old boys I knew as a young guy. There were Reg and Gordon, then Donny, Arthur, Jack, Eric; all of them a similar age to my dad. Dad was not able to help me directly, but at least gave me moral support. Another good old boy was Frank, a fairly successful local builder, and a bit of a hard guy. I knew him from years gone by, when I bought a couple of old terraced houses from him in my refurbishment days. After the Transit van died totally, I needed transport to work with. Frank had a one ton Mazda pickup truck, which was newish, and Frank wanted £800 for it. When I told him I did not have the cash, he told me to take the truck and pay him when I could. It took only about three months to pay him off, and I remember him with fondness for his kindness. As you might imagine, he had been in similar difficulties, throughout his life.

I still had very limited business acumen, but when I discovered solar heating I was confident that this would be the big one. It seemed the ideal product to build a direct selling company around. I set up the Solar Centre in the spring of 1976. My aforementioned 'sit in a darkened room' scenario was developed later, when I had a lot more to lose.

If anyone has ever been a little ahead of their time, this must rank with the best of them. I was ahead by some thirty years. Never to be fazed, my marketing concept was to organise and advertise solar heating exhibitions in hotels. I built some very basic stands and explanatory schematic drawings, and set about recruiting commission-only salesmen. This was surely to be the next big direct sales product, and I was in at the very start. My Father-in-Law worked as a lab assistant at Nottingham University and knew of a young doctor who specialised in all types of ecological innovations. Doctor Hanby conducted some technical training for my new sales guys. He also added certain credibility to my venture. After I sold and installed several solar systems it became clear that the UK was not ready, and the weather was not conducive to the maximisation of efficiency of these primitive systems. At one exhibition I held in Leicester an Italian man called Antonio Gravilli visited the stand. Antonio had a successful hairdressing business, and was about five years older than me. We became friends and had similar traits when it came to ambition. Tony convinced me that we should introduce my solar systems to southern Italy, his home district. In September 1976, I bought a Ford Granada on HP, I loaded it up with solar demonstration units, and along with Tony and my wife, I set off on the 2020 mile drive to Tora Suda.

After the miseries of the previous year, the feelings of emancipation and excitement when driving through the glorious countryside in Switzerland was indescribable. The three of us arrived in Antonio's brother's house in the early hours of the morning. The Italian family ethos is a sight to behold; they were so hospitable, it was utterly delightful. The venture failed and was probably the major reason why I began researching the fundamentals of marketing. If we had done any market research, we might have discovered that Italy is very hot, and the demonstration unit worked brilliantly. What we got wrong, was that Italians use cool water instead of hot, and shower rather than have a bath. The economics were a non-starter at that time.

There are five components to a business plan:

1. The concept.
2. The research of the project concept.
3. The actual written business plan, including the market, the competition, the dynamics, and all associated issues.
4. The breakdown of the business plan, to include a budget, cash flow forecast, and all financial matters.
5. A programme to commencement.

Following the aborted solar idea, Tony and I had some very enjoyable times shipping dilapidated antiques which we bought in the UK, then sold on and delivered to some great guys in Italy who owned a furniture restoration factory. Again, we made some money for a while, and had some fun at the same time.

Edenstone Builders, my new company selling and fixing showers and bathrooms, was turning over about £10,000 per month which allowed Carol and I to have a decent life, and to do some serious partying. All the time I was looking out for the next opportunity to appear.

In the summer of 1978, I was approached by a company called Hepworth Industrial Plastics. I was invited along with several others to attend a seminar. They were a big plastic pipe manufacturer, and had developed a product for the manufacture of uPVC windows and doors. Hepworth's were looking to promote this new innovation through the process of holding these seminars, which were in fact glorified piss-ups. Nonetheless, I did recognise the possible benefits to the householder, over and above the conventional materials of wood and aluminium.

Was this to be the product for me to build my selling company around? Two years later I started the making of my fortune with Synseal. •

SYNSEAL – THE BIRTH

When attending the seminar at Hepworth's Industrial Plastics, it was mentioned by the speaker that they were producing some fairly orthodox sales presentation folders. These were the usual point of sale aids, which all salesmen use.

Ever the opportunist, I enquired as to the cost the agency was charging for these presenters. I then offered to produce them at a lower price, and immediately received an order for 1000. The folders comprised about twenty printed sheets, with features and benefits of the uPVC window system. In addition, there were 42 actual photographs in each folder. These were not reproductions but real prints. The photos were stuck onto the papers adjacent to the appropriate text; all contained inside the normal foolscap plastic folder, with the clear Perspex leaves.

Having got the order, I had to set about making them up. I bought the 1000 folders from the old stationery firm I had worked for as a kid and had the 20 x thousand sheets printed by the print firm I usually used. Then came the 42,000 photos. Fortunately I had a friend in the photo lab business, and he arranged to have the heap of prints produced by a firm in Liverpool. After this, it came to assembling the whole job. Putting the sheets in the folders was boring work, but not anywhere near as dull

HAPPY HOLIDAYS

as sticking 42,000 photos to the paper sheets. I employed the whole family and some friends, for days. Bear in mind this was prior to the marvellous invention of Pritt. With that, it would still have been a major operation, but using doublesided Sellotape was a nightmare. After hours of ripping the backing off the tape we all had blood under our fingernails.

Anyway, the consignment was completed, and I put the whole lot in the back of my car which, at that time, was a Pontiac Transam. When I arrived at Hepworth's, they paid me and showed me round the window profile department. It had come on in leaps and bounds, and the product market penetration had gone up from less than 1% to nearly 2%. Great. I made about £1000 after all expenses, and Carol and I had a short holiday on the strength of this.

WHERE SYNSEAL STARTED

The following year, I received another order, and again in 1979. Clearly the folders were going to help the ever increasing numbers of salesmen sell the windows and doors, and by this time the penetration had risen to nearly 5% market share. At this time, I had moved my office away from Nottingham, owing to being fed up with travelling back and forth, and I rented a corner shop in Sutton-in-Ashfield. This was used as a base for my shower, bathroom and small building works company, Edenstone Ltd. I had little idea what to use the rest of the shop for, but I just thought something would occur. For several months I considered starting a cheap shoe shop, a three piece suite business, and a motorbike showroom.

After seeing the potential in uPVC windows – that was it! I mentioned earlier that timing is important in any enterprise, and I was convinced that the product had legs, as they say. Similarly, I have tried to avoid being a pioneer. In the old West, most pioneers got dead. In business, the mortality rate of pioneer companies is too high for my liking. So the product was now semi-proven, I thought, but still retained an embryonic aspect; just what I wanted, to create my direct selling company.

While on the subject of timing and enterprise, you may have noticed my avoidance of the word entrepreneur. This is because I regard the word as incorrectly used. It is glamorous and many people like to be regarded as entrepreneurs. I see it as a little like the days when industrial strikers called themselves 'wild cat strikers', and folks who try to thwart road expansions by burying themselves in the ground, saying they are 'eco warriors'. In my opinion both these types of people were simply a bloody nuisance, and with fairly limited intelligence levels. Mostly, entrepreneurs are seen as gamblers and serious risk takers. Though I am called an entrepreneur, I do not regard myself as a risk taker in the accepted sense of the expression. I am a risk manager, not a gambler. The word 'entrepreneur', when translated, is 'enterpriser'. Maybe it does not have the same 'je ne sais quoi' as 'entrepreneur', but nonetheless, that's what it means in English. If you like, generally speaking, all business people are entrepreneurs, and all entrepreneurs are business people.

On the question of timing, it is equally as important to know when the time arrives to get out of something, as it is to identify the time for innovation and enterprise.

Many a potentially decent business has foundered due to arrogance, pride or similar human frailties. One more of my homespun sayings fits well here:

"WHEN THE AMBER LIGHT COMES UP, DON'T WAIT FOR THE RED"

This scenario is not too dissimilar to many profitable companies going under due to cash flow difficulties.

Back to the story again. I had hitherto always steered clear of double glazing in any form, as this was at the lower end of a salesman's list of preferred products to sell. It had a poor reputation in the eyes of the public at large. My tactic to counter this image was to turn the shop I had into a showroom. This gave credibility to the business I intended to set up. It would give clients somewhere to go and pay their bills and, God forbid, somewhere to go if they had complaints or problems with installations. I had my joiners, who could easily transfer to fitting uPVC windows. I employed my late beloved brother to work for me, and his first job was to decorate the very shabby shop.

I had an older salesman with me at the time, whose name was Robin Everard. Robin was a nice man and being some 20 years older than me, provided a certain sounding board. He and I were all set to go off to London to seek out a company that was already manufacturing windows and doors from the uPVC extrusion. Before we left, Robin reminded me that he knew of a company in his old neck of the woods, Kettering in Northants. The company was called Graham Holmes Plastics, and they were manufacturing frames from Hepworth's profile extrusion, under the brand name of Astraseal. We called at Graham Holmes works on the way to London. The two principals were very pleasant and helpful men called Andy McKeon and Peter Barringham. Obviously, they were interested in selling the frames to me, and helped me considerably in the early days of Synseal.

After agreeing a deal, Robin and I saw no point in proceeding to London, so went off and had a marvellous luncheon at a good hotel in Kettering. I was becoming ever more excited with the prospect of the new game. As I mentioned previously, Edenstone was turning over about 10K per month and when I saw the sales chart at Graham Holmes with 63K for the month, I really did think that I had at last found what I had been looking for, ever since leaving school.

When my brother Stewart had completed the decoration, we had our new supplier give us a number of mismeasured frames, which were perfect for dressing out the showroom. I had pictures of Graham Holmes installations taken, and was delighted to see my showroom come together.

Now I addressed the matter of the opening, and the generation of interest in the area, for people to come in and see this revolutionary new product. The open day was set as the Easter Sunday of 1980. Perhaps quite a ballsy move was to take a double page spread in the local paper, in full colour. The £250 may not seem a lot today, but when you have nothing, it most certainly is. I arranged credit, to give me a chance to produce some sales and deposits to meet the invoice. The other method of primitive marketing I adopted was printing out leaflets on an old

Gestetner Machine, which had a winding handle, then distributing them throughout the district.

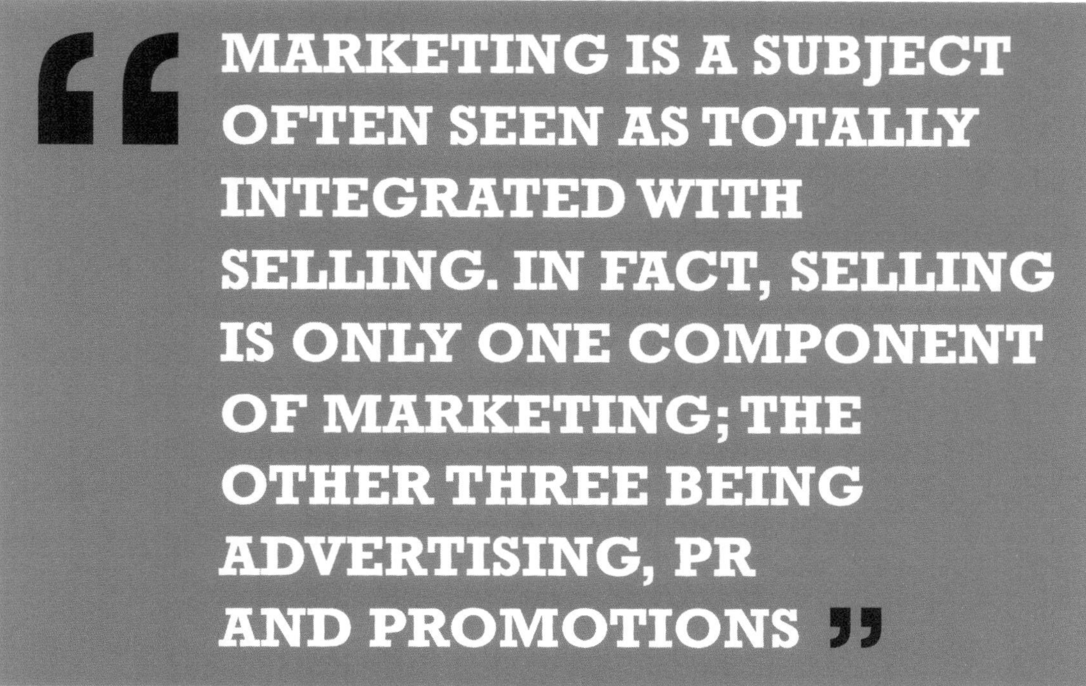

I have always considered theory to be essential, otherwise how do you know how to repeat, correct or analyse the progress of the business? Even now, I refer to the theory when considering a new project. It has stood me well.

Over the years that followed, Synseal became one of the most aggressive sales and marketing lead companies anywhere. I believe that our ever-increasing and sophisticated marketing has been a major reason for the success. My son Nick was ten years old when I started Synseal, and he became one of the best marketeers I have ever known. He is a good salesman. Not quite as good as I was in my prime, but

when it comes to marketing, he is better. He had patience to roll out the strategies, whereas I was always seeking rapid results.

Where did the name Synseal come from? Robin and I were in a pub called the Lord Byron, and I wanted to include the word 'seal' to ride on the back of Astraseal. Robin suggested Plastiseal, and I rejected it as sounding cheap. Over two more drinks, I said 'Synseal' as in Synthetic, and that was it. We had the name, and Easter Sunday drew ever nearer.

On the day, we opened at 10am, and Stewart, Robin, me, my wife, and former sister-in-law Ann, were waiting for the first person to come through the door. The girls had prepared some cheese and wine to make the opening more of a celebration. Little did the visitors realise that behind the front shop, there was a total mess. We had no hot water, and had to boil a kettle to wash the limited number of glasses we had.

Then it started. At 10.15, the door opened and in came Mr and Mrs Andy Mathews. I had prepared a presentation technique for Robin, Stew and me. For me, this was easy as it was really something I had been doing for 14 years. I was now 30 years of age.

When we closed for the first day, I had 32 leads appointed, for me to visit and sell to. In the next 48 hours, I had sold over £10,000 worth of windows and doors. That evening we were elated; me more than anyone, as it was my baby, and I was overjoyed with the start.

To put the 10K sales in two days into perspective, one needs to take account of the fact that my company at the time, Edenstone, which of course was still paying the wages, was selling 10K per month of its goods. When I sold Synseal 29 years ten months and three weeks later, it was turning over 10K every 12 minutes.

People have often asked me if I ever expected the company to grow to become the market leader it was. My answer has always been that without doubt I expected and intended to be the best. I simply had to learn an awful lot more about being a businessman. •

BIG DECISION

Following the exciting start of Synseal, I began rolling out the usual direct selling model. By the Christmas after the opening, I had several salesmen, three or four fitting teams, Robin, brother Stew, and a young girl called Tracey as general clerk, receptionist, secretary and tea maker.

The lead generation methods were newspapers, and girls in stores, supermarkets and the like. These girls handed out leaflets, and showed shoppers the benefits of not only uPVC, but Synseal uPVC. This was against the backdrop of the showroom; that continued to pull in a nice steady stream of good quality enquiries. After these 9 months of trading, the business was turning over about £15,000 per week, and was able to pay its way and sustain me without the assistance of Edenstone Ltd, which I was still running alongside Synseal.

My accountant David was looking after my books one day each week, and we discussed the termination of Edenstone. Naturally, I was more interested in developing Synseal, and Edenstone was somewhat less than solvent. The upshot was that we called a creditors meeting in order to arrange a creditors voluntary liquidation of Edenstone. As the meeting was called in a hotel in Derby, a different town, on the afternoon of New Year's Eve, only one creditor turned up. The meeting was quite straightforward. I had, of course, had some experience in such matters a few years earlier.

The next stage was to develop Synseal, and increase the revenues. I decided to replicate the showroom concept, and found rented units at what I called the wrong end of the right street. This was Main Street, but not in the town centre. First, there was Nottingham, then Chesterfield, Ilkeston and Derby. Headquarters were still in the offices we had created above the shop in Sutton-in-Ashfield. By now, business had increased to over 20K per week, and was climbing quickly. We had more staff looking after the new showrooms, and we were constantly seeking more good salesmen.

At this juncture, it is appropriate to mention the matter of building infrastructures. In the Synseal business, at this time, it was ok to run as a one man band insofar as management went. Over this level, there needs to be the very basic infrastructure of necessary skills. This consists of the salesman, the bean counter, and the operation/ production guy. As always, timing is critical. Set on the people and incur the expenses too soon, and you may run out of money; too late, and the development will suffer. In my view, this very rudimentary infrastructure can be adequate from say £1M up to about £10M, but after that, a full-blown tiered management team is required, with Directors, senior managers, department heads, supervisors etc. It would be a while before I arrived at the dizzy heights of selling £200,000 of work each week.

Another of my business rules that I have come to live by is that:

“NO ONE PERSON SHOULD HAVE MORE THAN ABOUT 7 PEOPLE REPORTING TO HIM ON A DAILY BASIS”

Over the years, I developed this controlled management structure, and you will see that in essence, when I had 7 directors, and they each had 7 senior managers, and so on, it formed a pyramid system that worked. Needless to say, building the business often required some changes in specific personnel, but the basic formula remains good.

By now, I had learned more about the financial control essential to success, and introduced budgets, cash flows and monthly management accounts. Sounds obvious, but many companies don't know how they are progressing month on month. My personal commercial knowledge was growing, and I studied the niceties of direct costs, indirect costs, direct variables, and indirect variables. Funding came from bank overdrafts, which were then provided by Barclays, and a very pleasant and old style manager called Mike Page. We were operating very hand to mouth, and constantly monitoring our cash collections and expenditure. As my knowledge grew, I began to look for profit enhancement methods, and added value opportunities.

The next quantum step was to discontinue buying frames in from Graham Holmes Plastics and start manufacturing. This was a whole new ball game. My work was varied and plentiful, from around 8.30am until 9 at night. In the evening, I would be out training new sales recruits, or sat in the cold office, with a couple of telephone canvassers I had employed. In addition, I spent time learning and developing future strategies. Making our own frames would not only be more profitable, but would also improve the company image, and give us more credibility. Strategy was not the sort of word we used very often back in the beginning, but again, it is something crucial to the building of a successful business.

Too often, I find that the words strategy, policy and tactics are confused and misunderstood.

- **Strategy is a series of plans.**
- **Policies are the disciplines and rules to achieve the strategy.**
- **Tactics are the detailed methods of arriving at the given objective within the overall strategic plan.**

I was perhaps the least technically minded person, and really have remained so throughout the years. But that did not matter, with my conviction that all you need is to find a man that can, and incentivise him well. This man was to be Mr Malcolm Le Masurier.

Malc was not your orthodox sort of a fellow; he was 27 years of age, originally from Jersey in the Channel Islands. He was 6 feet four inches tall, and had hair and a beard that reached his trouser belt. He is 5 years younger than me, and attended an interview for the job of production manager. At this interview, Malc convinced me that he was the man I needed, although he was also the only applicant. At the time, Malcolm was working for Ashfield Glass, a long established manufacturer of aluminium windows that had recently moved into uPVC production and sales. They were well down the road of their expansion and turned out to be something of a competitor.

I took Malc to see the factory unit that I told him I was renting, which was a little overstatement, as I could not justify or afford the rent until I had my man to run it. The unit was completely empty: no air lines, benches or anything. The arrangement was that Malcolm would get back to me in a day or so to confirm his acceptance of the job, and his starting date. Not having ever been blessed with patience, I decide to precipitate Malc's move by calling his then employer, Ashfield Glass, and having Malcolm called to speak to me on the factory loud speaker system. That meant he became persona non gratis at Ashfield Glass! The public announcement of Gary Dutton from Synseal calling him was too much for his then bosses, and his position there was untenable. Having helped him to decide to join me, Malc started on July 27th 1981. To this day, he reminds me of my sneaky method of his recruitment, but he does say, it proved one hell of a good move in the decades that followed.

In line with our policy of holding opening events, the 2,400 sq foot factory was opened in the summer of 1981. As with the inaugural showroom opening, it was another resounding success.

Over the next couple of years, it was consolidation and development combined. We had a very simple business model, and proceeded to augment the company's activities with more showrooms being opened. This meant more sales staff, more fitting teams and admin staff. There were ever more lead generating methods introduced. One of these was to buy an old single decked bus, which I had converted and signwritten to be a mobile showroom. This was a great success, and the sales guys and gals used it to good effect at country shows and ideal home exhibitions.

By way of an update on the state of play, it was now 1983, and we were moving ahead. We had outgrown the factory, and went into a new unit which was rented with an option to buy. We built offices there, and moved the HQ from above the shop into this new factory. Brother Stewart had decided to leave my employ, and actually went to work for Ashfield Glass for a while. Sadly he found working for his brother not to his liking, but it was a little galling to see him go to the competition.

Although the infrastructure was not yet totally formalised in terms of titles, there was an embryonic management team. I was now the Managing Director, Malc was the production chief, Graham Webster was in charge of sales and David was doing more and more in the area of financial control and accounts. By the mid 80's we had 14 showrooms in 5 counties throughout the Midlands, some 40 sales guys and a dozen or so fitting teams. Computers were introduced into most areas of the operation, and then came another defining moment, and one which always stays with me.

Whilst expanding to the position described, David worked full time with Synseal as Finance Director. He knew as well as I did the constant difficulties we had funding our growth. Having sold his accountancy practice, he came and suggested that he should have a share in the equity of Synseal, and offered several thousands of pounds for 40% of the business. The company was still functioning from hand to mouth and his offer was realistic in terms of valuation. The injection of cash would have been just what the doctor ordered, but I rejected David's offer. It turned out to be one of my best decisions ever, and provided the bedrock for what was to become yet another of my commercial convictions. The idea of partners in any form has increasingly become complete anathema to me.

As years went by, I realised increasingly that I needed to make about 6 or 7 major decisions each year, but by God, I had to get them right. As my knowledge grew, my policies developed, and I learned the skills of evolving from salesman to sales manager, to sales director to managing director.

In my chosen way, I need to have the theory behind things. It is my belief that the job of a director is to contribute to the creation and monitoring of company strategy and policy. It is the MD's job to manage the directors' activities. More recent years have seen me performing the function of chairman of the board, which entails the four primary functions of heading the company, protecting the company, representing the company, and maintaining a consensus between the directors.

The matter of taxation appeared when we made our first meaningful profit in one year. The concept of grafting like I did and then giving money away was completely abhorrent to me. A man by the name of Philip, working with one of the big four firms of accountants told me, "Pay it, forget it, and get on with making some more; that's what you're good at."

Sound advice, that I have followed with some reluctance ever since. In the years between 2008 and 2010, I personally paid £15,000,000 in CGT alone. This was on top of all the normal income tax, and after much heavy duty tax structuring to mitigate the charges.

PARTY HOUSE '85

It was 1986 when Carol, Nick and I built our first house; it was big, and a great party house, and we sure did party.

As things developed, it became necessary for me to accede to Malcolm's request that I forsake my normal practice of personally opening all the mail received each day: tons of it. My work function had changed, and often I did not arrive at the office until 9 am. I considered that opening the mail was an excellent way of keeping tabs on the general goings on in the business. Malc told me that this process was causing hold-ups in the areas of order processing. So there it was. I handed over this responsibility to my secretary.

Relationships inevitably develop in one's working life, and by way of a word of warning, there was a very difficult period that transpired around this time. Some of the girls working in a business find perceived power and success attractive. I was not a bad looking guy, but I was No Brad Pitt. The point I am making is that I was busy, tired to a point, and totally focused on my business; I truly did not see it coming. The long and short of it was that a silly affair ensued and the consequence of this major mistake was that I went into a very dark place for quite some time.

I recall that Graham Webster came into my office one morning and said, "Hey boss, don't jump on me for what I am about to say, but if you catch a cold round here the rest of us get fucking pneumonia. So can you please get your act together?"

There I am, thinking nobody knew, and really it was clear that I had temporarily lost the plot. There was only one cure, I had no desire to become divorced from Carol, and chose the only option open to me: say goodbye to the girl and tell my wife. The following times were difficult to say the least, but after a while, and much 'Gary-bollocking,' we settled down. Be aware, all you would-be business men, of the honey trap.

Around 1988, I acknowledged that there were sea changes occurring in the window and door industry, as were the routes to market: the home owner. From my days as a direct salesman I knew that all products have an ephemeral life expectancy in the direct sell world.

The bespoke nature of windows and doors had significantly extended this period, but changes were a-coming. We had now seen off most of the serious competition in our area of activity, mainly due to our focus on aggressive sales and marketing. The fundamental tenet of direct sell products is that they must have a certain mystique in order to maintain their premium price level. When they become more everyday items, and are available to be price checked very easily, it transpires that the sales guys are denied the opportunity to promote the value of the guarantee, and the quality of work provided by a 'big company'. The prospective client simply says something like, "Well, my mother had John and Jack change her windows recently and she's very happy."

So there it was: two men in a van were taking over big slabs of the end-user market.

It was at this time that we decided to start manufacturing windows and doors for the 'trade'. The trade was largely made up of fitters and salesmen who had once worked for firms such as Synseal, and then gone off and set up on their own. With few or no expenses and working for wages, the price levels to the end user were plummeting. Between '88 and '89, we ran both divisions in tandem, but with the increasing emphasis on trade. Not only was I of the mind that the future was in trade sales, but we were also suffering problems running with the hare and the hounds. By this I mean we were competing with our trade customers through our own retail sales activities. Something had to happen.

One Wednesday morning, after a fairly sleepless night thinking about the next move, it came to me like a bolt from the blue. Having got up and done some sums, I rang my team of directors and announced that I wanted them to meet me for breakfast at the nearby Swallow Hotel. When they arrived, I quickly apprised them of my view on the current situation, and in the main they agreed with my comments.

Then I dropped the bomb: "We are going to close the retail side on Friday this week."

GETTING ON WITH BUILDING THE BUSINESS

I believe one of my abilities is to surround myself not only with talented guys, but also strong people. I have always felt that bosses who need sycophants have a serious character flaw. The close-down project had to be swift and positive in order to avoid the word spreading, creating a chaotic situation in which company property would go missing, and all sorts of other undesirable situations might occur.

It was organised like a military campaign. Between the hours of 8am and noon, we had synchronised the dismissal of all the sales staff, all the promo staff, all the fitting teams, and above all else, the closing and lock-changing of 14 showrooms through the Midlands. Brutal? Yes. Ruthless? Yes. Necessary for the greater good? Absolutely, and without doubt.

Synseal would now begin its next incarnation: to become the country's leading manufacturer of windows and doors to the trade. At its height, we would be making 2500 units each week. •

START OF EXTRUSION

BUSINESS BUILDING

Now, in 1990, and with the business totally focused on the trade sale of windows and doors, one of my directors, Clive, left me under acrimonious circumstances. Clive had too many outside problems, he became very antagonistic and disruptive, and I was left with no choice but to fire him.

He had left Bowater following a scam, which had been promoted by Clive's then boss, the Bowater group CEO. Clive and I were encouraged by this gentleman to attempt to secure a deal with a small PLC based in Grimsby, UK. The deal entailed me fronting the owner of the company with an offer to buy it. The CEO of Bowater told us he could not make the approach directly. After I had secured an option to buy the company, I developed some misgivings. These were vindicated after I challenged the CEO, and it turned out that he was not acting on behalf of Bowater. He, I heard, was summarily dismissed, and Clive was also tainted for his apparent naivety and had no future with Bowater, so he came and joined me at Synseal.

During our trips to Europe, I managed to acquire a taste for cognac. This became serious when I started to lose the ability to put the top back on the bottle. In 1990, I stopped taking the top off at all, and have never drunk brandy again, to this day.

My dad found himself out of work. Knowing he was a good salesman, I offered him a job, which lasted for six years, until he became somewhat irascible and out of step with the other senior people on the firm. I 'retired' him against his wishes when he was 67.

I looked for a new MD to take over half of my role of Chairman and MD. Ideally, I wanted someone with a reputation in the industry and hopefully someone with a dowry of customers that he could bring with him. By coincidence the man I selected, Alex, had also been a director of Bowater.

Alex was a decent enough and capable man, but without the dynamism that has become the creed of Synseal. Alex did not cut the mustard as MD, and I reinstated myself in the role, moving him to sales director. He was later replaced in this position, in favour of my son, Nick. Nick was still in his twenties but had developed into a formidable marketing man with considerable people skills. Clearly the two years of supporting him through Business College had paid off.

Any business has its own unique idiosyncracies. With the trade sales operation, it was credit exposure to customers. We suffered some serious bad debts, and therefore became very fastidious over credit control. Following two serious hits for many thousands of pounds, Malc and I were have a Boxing Day pint, and ridiculing the ease with which companies could set up and then go into a pre-pack liquidation.

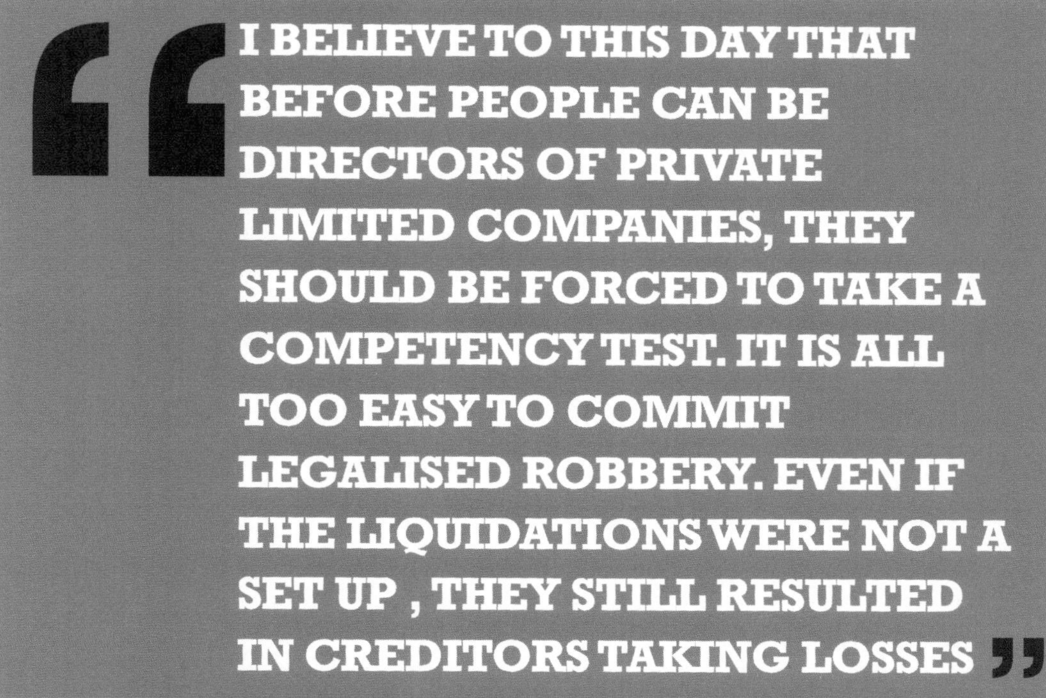

I should know. I was, once upon a time, a director of businesses that went under.

After the discussion on this subject, Malcolm and I talked about the next improvement to Synseal, and determined that this should be through vertical integration, whereby instead of buying in profile extrusions, we would continue the design of our own window systems, and set up our own extrusion facility. This entailed major capital investment, and additional premises. I remember others thinking at the time that this enterprise was either very brave or very stupid. In reality it was neither, since we had an in-house requirement for extrusion sufficient to utilise two extrusion lines

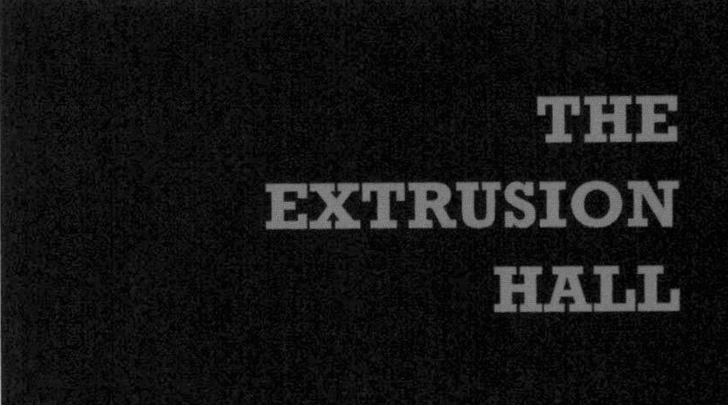
THE
EXTRUSION
HALL

and reduce costs, therefore making more profit. The intention, however, was to become a serious player in selling our profile extrusion to the type of companies of which we had been customers, up to that point.

Off we went, and bought a couple of extrusion lines at a cost of £250,000 each. Next came the recruitment of the men with the expertise to run this new area of the business. After some false starts with staffing, the extrusion division began to rock and roll. More extrusion lines were needed, with more demands for capital for expansion. After years with Barclays, came the salutary lesson: I don't deal with the institution; only the individual. The old manager, Mick Page, had retired now we had some hopeless young fool who could not run a bath, let alone a bank. Our relationship was never good, and after this fool declared that my industry had an image below that of second-hand car dealers, I responded that this might be so, but the image was still superior to that of moneylenders - i.e. banks. After that, we had to find a new bank.

Another tip when business building:

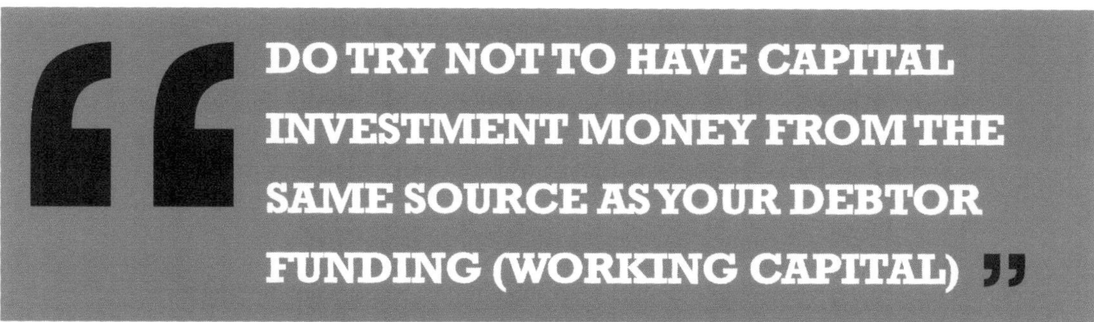

Inevitably, the funder will regard the two in aggregate, and if the going gets tough, the lender will be more likely to call in some or all of the monies borrowed.

Eventually, after much work, we made the acquaintance of Dennis from the NatWest banking group. We were looking for a £250,000 overdraft facility and when Dennis announced that he would not lend us this amount, we were crestfallen. In the next sentence he said he would grant a £500,000 overdraft. Later Dennis became a director of the bank; in part, no doubt, resulting from his visionary view of supporting promising businesses like Synseal, wherein he ensured that the directors were not preoccupied with the day to day problems of cash shortage.

At about the same time as we started extrusion activities in 1992, I had my first real insight into the world of The City. Always wanting to improve my knowledge of the commercial world in general, I was disposed to buy what were then described as 'option contracts'. These days they are called derivatives. I bought 25 lots of 25 tonnes each of aluminium through the city brokers, and when we were waiting for the London Metal Exchange to open at noon, I was cautiously excited. The excitement soon died as twelve seconds after the Exchange opened, the Tarquin (I call all city types 'Tarquins'), told me that I had 'cut out'. This meant that the price of aluminium had momentarily gone below the price at which I had, on their advice, chosen to restrict my potential loss. Therefore, I lost several thousands and was not a happy bunny. Ever since my foray with gambling as a teenage salesman, it was not to my liking, and this was just that: gambling. Observing that I was feeling not a little aggrieved at this situation, the Tarquin attempted to ingratiate himself by asking me to visit their dealing room. Having travelled to London for a 12 second horror, I said 'Okay'.

To this day I regard the lost money as well spent in the cause of my education. In the dealing room were a whole bunch of young guys shouting across the room at each other and gabbing into telephones. At one point, something to the effect of, "Get your clients off crude and on to soya!" was communicated around these guys.

Then followed some frantic calls to their respective clients, relaying this crock of crap. When I asked my chaperon, Tarquin, what this was all about, he replied in a serious tone, that it was all to do with an Arab sheik's son getting married or similar bollocks. To begin with, I thought he was taking the piss, but now I know this is a typical example of the workings of the markets. The price of crude had gone down and soya gone up – and why? There was absolutely no correlation in a rational or proper commercial sense. It was then that I realised that the markets do not conform to what I regard as normal commercial reality; they work on perception, which then results in reality. Bemused but wiser, I went home pleased not to be in this area of the commercial world. Maybe I am somewhat old fashioned. If so, then it works for me.

A few years later, I had another experience with the City which produced some further scepticism on the workings of such institutions. This was in 1994 when I decided that the extrusion business was the future and I was looking for a payday. The event was the process of looking to float my business on the UK stock exchange. •

MILLIONAIRE TIME

By now, the Synseal methodology was becoming more sophisticated, and I held monthly management meetings, in which all current important issues were on the agenda I produced. There was always a final section for AOB (Any Other Business) to provide the opportunity for the other directors to table their particular points. I have always tried to run a fairly open policy, where everyone knows what is happening, and what their part in it is.

Some say I run a benevolent dictatorship, and some say a dictatorial democracy; whichever it is, it works. I developed, in my own management style, a simple method of getting a result. When looking at new budgets, I used my knowledge of the company, the competition, the economic macro and micro situations, and came up with what was fundamentally a desired bottom right hand corner figure. This was the pre-tax profit I would like to anticipate. We would hold the budget meeting and look through the SWOT (Strength, Weaknesses, Opportunities and Threats) analysis.

I tried to be as realistic as possible, and then asked the guys "What do you want, to produce this number?" After much discussion, there was invariably a consensus, meaning that the target I set was feasible, and the directors were, in the main, granted the facilities and resources to take us the next level. The benefit of this method is clear: if I provided the wherewithal requested, and if three months later the results were not forthcoming, then the guys had no one to blame but themselves. It is not a perfect system, but I know of many that are inferior.

Synseal was now serious player in both trade frame extrusion supply as well as trade frame market; the turnover was growing, and having run the business for nearly 15 years, it came to the time where I wanted to get some serious money in my own pocket. What I certainly did not want, was to sell up completely and not have a business remaining. At this time, we were now with Coopers and Lybrand Accountants, and they introduced me to the merchant bank with which they worked closely, Singer and Friedlander.

My two main contacts were John and Mike at Coopers and Singers respectively.

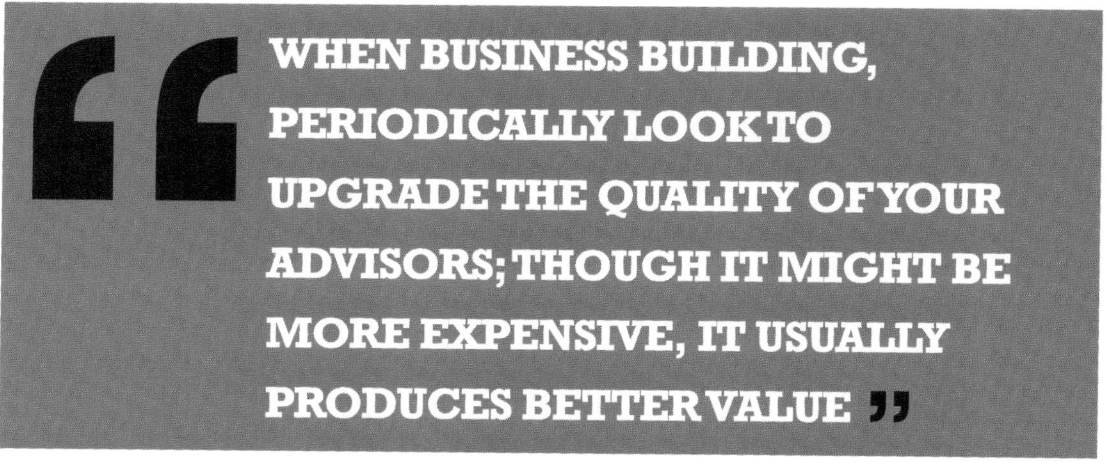

In the words of the great Warren Buffett:

"PRICE IS WHAT YOU PAY; VALUE IS WHAT YOU GET"

As usual, I am looking forward, not only to the result of the floatation idea, but also the new dimension I expect to be added to my career. I can honestly say that I did learn a lot throughout the process, but not what I originally expected. At the first exploratory meeting held at Singers offices in Nottingham, there was John, Mike and me; the wine flowed, and the lunch in the private dining room was great. I came away thinking this was to be the next big chapter, and over the next few months Coopers and Lybrand set about producing the Long Form report on Synseal. This cost me 250K, but it was all part of the process.

The social side of the relationship developed, and Carol and I were invited to Ascot race meetings, the best golf clubs (I am a shit golfer), and the country's top shooting estates (I am not a shit shot). This, I learned, is all part of the nurturing process when a company is being groomed for floatation. There were invitations to the Singer and Friedlander house in London, and get-togethers at other venues. It was after several months, that I was introduced to the intended City brokers. I was advised to appoint to the board of Synseal two non-executive directors. The two guys were from the 'professions': one solicitor, and one accountant. These chaps were pleasant, but really brought nothing to the party. Their sole purpose was to 'educate' us on the requirements of becoming a publicly quoted company. I remember reading a quote from the late Tiny

Rowland of Lonrho Plc; he said non-execs are as much use as tinsel on a Christmas tree. Following my experience, I do tend to share this view.

After many huge meetings with the advisors, and the appointment of my own corporate lawyers, Browne Jacobson, the project was becoming extremely time-consuming. Me being an orthodox type of businessman, I was constantly reminding people that we still had to run Synseal and not become totally consumed by the floatation. At one of the meetings, my FD, David, was embarrassed by the quantum of information he was required to produce. The FD is crucial to the process, and David increasingly appeared to be less than comfortable with his new workload. He was a capable company accountant, but this was a whole new ballgame. The City people involved were not too dissimilar in mentality and style to those I had come across when losing money buying option contracts. I don't see these people as business builders; they are manipulators. But I had an objective, and as I hold the view that the end justifies the means – within reason – then I had no problem tolerating most of these new circumstances.

Following on, was the first of several situations, in which I thought "What the hell am I doing?"

At a meeting with one Tarquin, he said he thought I paid my directors too much. He was a kid in his early twenties, and had little or no experience outside the city. Somewhat aggravated, I retorted that if he could find me some replacement directors who were as good at half the price, I would have a bunch of them. Tarquin did not see the sarcasm or the point I was making. By way of elaboration, I asked him what would he prefer, "To pay 50k, and earn a million? Or pay 100k and earn two million?"

MALC AND ME
AFTER A HARD
DAY AT SEA 1991

I'LL HAVE WHAT GARY DUTTON IS HAVING...

Gary Dutton, the gung-ho king of PVC windows and conservatories, is blowing away the competition. He tells **Charles Orton-Jones** how to deal with trade unions, greedy directors, and City boys "who couldn't run a bath".

10 **REAL BUSINESS** NOVEMBER 2004

If you ever meet Gary Dutton you will find him refreshingly different. Take his attitude to staff relations. When unions threatened to recruit the workforce at his PVC window and conservatory frames firm Synseal four years back, Dutton faced them down.

Needless to say, Dutton is not your typical company chairman. Today Synseal has 700 employees and a 19% market share in conservatories. Dutton reckons that next year they will be market leaders- and it's hard to doubt this. Synseal's turnover for the past five years has gone from £29m to £85m. Profits have leapt from £2m to £16m over the same period. And Dutton, you'll note, still owns 100 per cent.

Talking to him is a revelation. In his broad Notts accent he answers every question with a directness and honesty that has been expunged from most modern boardrooms.

Dutton runs Synseal his own way. With no formal business training he's developed his own homespun business philosophy. Some of this thinking is ingenious, such as his Seven Man Rule: "I believe that each man should have no more than seven people reporting to him. I've got my seven directors, and they've got seven people below them, and so on.

PHOTOGRAPHY: NICK DAWE

The logic of my equation seemed to go completely over his head. Increasingly, I was coming to doubt whether I could tolerate a future in the world of 'Woolf Reforms', 'Cadbury', and all the other areas of bureaucracy involved in going public. The prospect of at least £10,000,000 in my pocket on day one, and a lot more further down the road, kept my interest for a time. The plan was to float on what is called a 'forecast'. This intention was to offer on the market in November, and as our year end was March, it would include a forecast of the year-end profits.

We were now at the beauty parade stage, where we did the tour of the institution managers, looking to generate interest in investing in the Synseal PLC business. I was the one to be presenting the basic benefits of this investment, and I would be introduced and accompanied by one of the brokers.

My companion was a tall fellow with a background of Eton, the Guards, and then the City. Beautifully spoken, and apparently well connected, he was nevertheless daft in what he suggested. His idea was that we present the case to the fund managers we were to visit on the basis that the forecast for the second half year's performance of Synseal would be superior to the first half of the fiscal year. I was astounded and said something to the effect of, "Are these people all stupid? For the last fourteen years, the first half of the year has been better than the second, and in any case, the second half has two less weeks in it!"

It was right there and then, that I decided to abort the whole process. I called in Mike and John, and told them that I was 'pulling' the deal. They went away not happy, but in no position to do anything about it. I was relieved and enlightened, but it did cost a lot, both in monetary terms and indirectly. David, my FD, had suffered through the process, and virtually had a nervous breakdown; he left Synseal shortly afterwards following some further issues. This was not a question of him doing anything untoward, but more a matter of him being shot to hell. Although David and I are not in contact these days, it is fair to say he was invaluable in the early times, and I still regard him with considerable fondness.

Not unsurprisingly, the invitations to various social events ceased with immediate effect.

Back to square one; still running my successful company, and still looking for a pay day for Gary Dutton.

1995, and I set about trying to find a buyer for the part of the company that was manufacturing the finished frames. I had kept the two sides of the business separate, in case I did want to break off one side or the other. The conflict happened again, as in the past: Synseal was selling its frames in the same market as our profile extrusion customers; as such it was not good for the development of extrusion sales.

I invited Mike and John to assist and advise on seeking out a buyer for the part of my business that made and sold frames to the trade. Six months went by, and I became more and more frustrated with the clandestine methods they used to promote the deal. In the autumn, I told them that I was going to put an ad in the Financial Times. They were totally aghast; their way was to be less overt.

"But," said I, "I am the salesman here, and contrary to my usual preference for a rifle type of marketing approach, I feel spread shot marketing is appropriate in this situation."

We received 32 enquiries from the advert, and filtered out the tyre kickers and sightseers, leaving about ten prospects, to whom we would offer all the appropriate information, in an attempt to sell the business.

I recall executives from one big firm involved in the wood trade coming along. They were very interested, but after an initial look round my works, they came into my office and announced that they would not be proceeding with their interest. Me being the old time salesman, challenged their announcement. There then followed the best backhanded compliment I think I have ever received. The reason for the abandonment of interest, was that they had expected to find that they could introduce improvements to Synseal, in order to add value if they bought it. But they couldn't find fault. Their honesty was a little brutal; but quite simply they thanked me, and said they were going back to their business armed with some Synseal methods to improve their own existing practices.

Eventually, I received an offer of £3,250,000 for the business from JBS Industries. After much legal wrangling, posturing and sparring, deal day was decided to be 1st of December 1995.

I ensured that I learned a lot about this type of deal, and in order to make sure that all the lawyers on the buyer's side knew that it was my game, and that we would play by my rules, I told them that I would not tolerate the final details being dragged on into the small hours of the morning. This tactic is used by the lawyers to justify their fee, to demonstrate their expertise, and to weaken the decision makers into making inappropriate compromises. As a bit of grandstanding, I told one of the JBS solicitors that I did not want an electronic transfer of the

ME, SAT NEXT TO ONE OF MY HEROES: SIR JOHN HARVEY-JONES

consideration money, but I wanted a bank draft. He superciliously asked why, and I told him I wanted to show it to my mother.

He rudely replied, "Will your mother know what a bank draft is?" Not to be out done by a solicitor, I finished by saying, "Maybe she won't, but she can count the noughts on the draft."

Deal done at 1 pm, we all went off to the Swallow Hotel, for the traditional celebrations. Malc got completely pissed, and I was now a millionaire. With my previous tax planning and restructuring, there was no CGT to pay, this time. Over the weekend, Carol and I sat drinking champagne, and drinking in the achievement. It was great to be financially safe and looking forward to the future. The immediate future included building another house in Carol's beloved Newstead Abbey grounds, expanding

Synseal's extrusion activities, and taking our first trip to the Caribbean. This trip was to be fantastic, and was made all the better by supersonic travelling on Concorde! The fascinating part of supersonic travel was taking off from Heathrow at 9am and arriving in Barbados at 8.55am (five minutes before we took off, with a four hour time difference.)

> **"IF ANYONE GOES SKINT AFTER HAVING 3.25 MILLION POUNDS, THEY ARE EITHER STUPID OR A GAMBLER. I DO NOT CONSIDER MYSELF TO BE EITHER"**

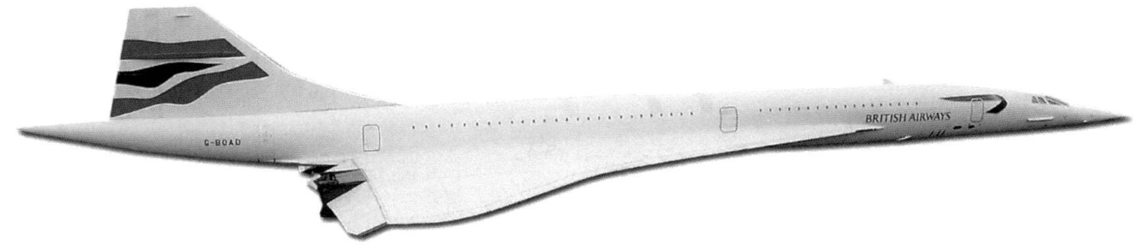

TAKING STOCK

So where am I now? 45, a sort of mini multi-millionaire, with a good wife, good son, beautiful house; reasonably well regarded, and, to a point, living within the confines of my own conscience. I don't suffer quite the same fluctuations between pseudo-euphoria and an adverse but similar degree of moroseness, but it is still there, not far below the surface. I try to hide my sensitivity, because that's what we tough-guy businessmen do. I am still driven by the fear of failure, and have never been a good loser. I still feel the need to prove that I am good at something, and business is what I do.

"SHOW ME A GOOD LOSER AND I WILL SHOW YOU A LOSER"

I genuinely need friendship, and that's where the next hard lesson raised its head. From having lots of so-called friends, I find myself somewhat lonely,

and with a very much shrunken circle of friends. But then again, maybe I never had that many. Maybe it was just me, thinking they were friends. I don't really blame some folks for deserting me, as such. Some thought they could not keep up with my new lifestyle, some were just jealous and others resented me. I never lost the value of friends; nor did I lose the value of a pound.

"THERE ARE ONLY TWO BASIC MOTIVATORS: THE FEAR OF LOSS AND THE GREED OF GAIN; THE FORMER IS BY FAR THE MOST POWERFUL.

NOT BAD, FOR A COUNCIL HOUSE KID

At the time that I sold the piece of Synseal for £3.25M, and at this time of writing, a further 15 years on, with loads more cash in the tin, I reckon that I like extravagance, but not waste. These days, even with my yacht in the Med, private jet travel, and fleet of magnificent cars, there is still the underlying something that makes me want to keep going and building.

For some time in the eighties I had what was like an adrenalin band around my head. I had to prove I was good at something.

Sometimes, for instance, in quiet moments, I think back to the times when I went to see a doctor who I thought was far enough away from where I lived and worked, for me to be anonymous. It was in the eighties, when I was in one of my dark periods. I hasten to add that these are less frequent nowadays, but still exist. Dr York was very understanding; he listened to me, and noticed that I had been to take a drink of water from his sink several times in the thirty minutes since I arrived in his surgery. He diagnosed me as being in some emotional mess, exhausted and burnt out. The surprise came when he told me that he knew who I was, what I did, and moreover he described the fact that I thought no one else could ever understand. He said that he knew of other people that I would be familiar with too, who had been in the same state of mind as I was. Of course, he said he could not tell me the names of these people, but he could tell me of one... Himself. I felt relief in the knowledge that I was not the only one. Dr York then told me that I was, as he explained, like a mouse on a wheel. I was working, going home, having rows with Carol and others, having one too many drinks, and then going back to work. The solution he recommended was to find something totally removed from my current life existence. I took his advice, and that weekend I drove to a marina on the River Trent. I had not been to the place since childhood, when I was there with my dad.

To help break the cycle that Dr York identified, I bought a boat on H.P. (Hire Purchase), and learned about boats and everything to do with them. My mind soaked up the information and lessons like a sponge; it was a sort of brainwash. Since those days, I have taken various exams, and now have the right to call myself Captain, as I am a qualified Yacht Master.

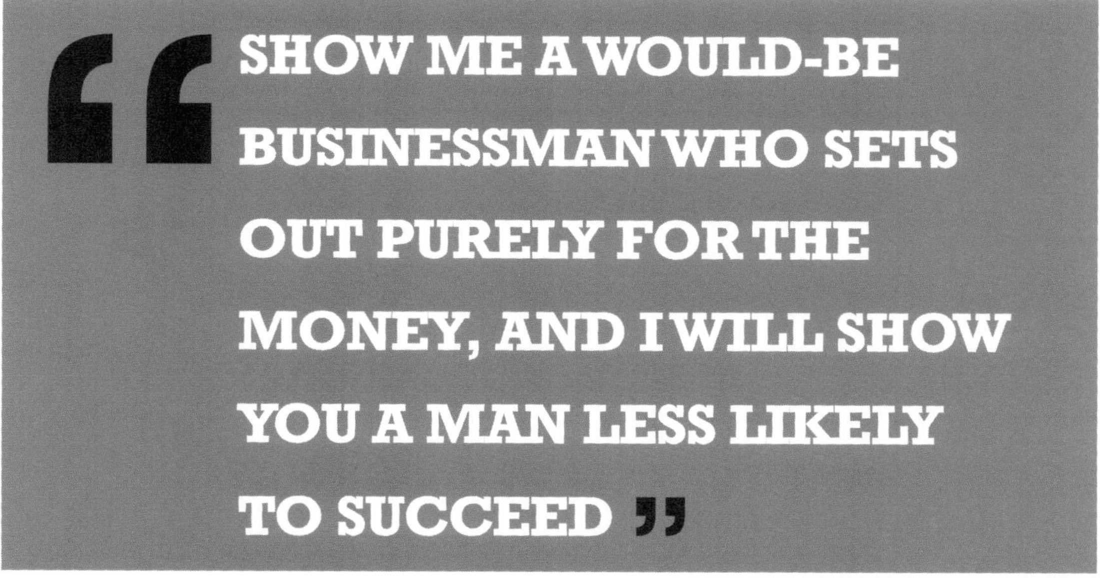

“SHOW ME A WOULD-BE BUSINESSMAN WHO SETS OUT PURELY FOR THE MONEY, AND I WILL SHOW YOU A MAN LESS LIKELY TO SUCCEED”

Money provides security and civility, in what I consider to be an increasingly uncivilised world. Before I graduated to private flying, I was likely to wind up being arrested in airports. The idea of being treated like an animal, as I see happen in airports today, was totally unacceptable. Being quite robust with my repartee, I was constantly becoming confrontational with the objectionable creatures employed as airport staff. Once, having asked one odious moron, “Did they employ you because you are a rude and ignorant, or were you trained to be that way?" I got close to being the victim of the Gestapo!

Not long after the 1995 deal completion, Carol and I were in London, and I had received an offer to sell the extrusion company. Carol, in all innocence, told me that she thought it would not be long after the recent deal, before I sold out altogether. How wrong she was. The offer of £12 million in 1996 was a non-starter as far as I was concerned, and it was my decision entirely. I didn't sell for many years, for reasons I will outline later.

The highs and lows have always affected me, but I grew more adept at hiding my feelings. As I said in the preface of this book, my journey has been, and will likely remain, one of emotional ups and downs.

I don't seem to struggle with commercial stress, and actually miss it when things are going pretty smoothly. I see stress as akin to inflation. Just as the economy needs some inflation to keep it moving, I need the stimulus of commercial stress to keep me motivated. An overdose in this analogy is not good, however.

I have grown to believe that a person's nature is something they are born with, genetic if you wish, and their character begins the moment one leaves mummy's womb. Perhaps people comprise of a bit of both; but for sure, there have been times that I wished I had been less driven, and not so much of a man on a mission.

I am a disciple of the John Slater (Slater Walker Investments) school of luck. I believe he coined the definition that: "Luck is when opportunity meets preparation". I try to be prepared to meet and greet opportunity. Though I often crave excitement, I need normality just as much, and occasionally I drive alone to the places I knew as a child. Not to keep my feet on the ground, but just for the nostalgia.

That's enough soul baring for the moment, so I will return to the matter of business building. Before I do, and just to endorse my point, if anyone reading this book finds themselves with similar personal dilemmas to those I have encountered, don't forget you are not the only one who's been there. It just feels like it, at the time. •

SILVER
WEDDING
ANNIVERSARY

1996

On the personal front, 1996 started very well. Carol and I had a wonderful first time experience in the Caribbean, made all the better for having seen the curvature of the earth on the return trip by Concorde from 60,000 feet in the air.

I was driving a Bentley turbo car, with a Range Rover for winter time, and my ever increasing interest was game shooting. I bought Carol a Mercedes sports car, and we had a brand new 42 foot sports cruiser berthed in the south of France in a port called Camille Rayon, just outside Cannes.

Coincidental with the sale of the fabrication business to JBS industries, we had found a 7 acre plot of land in Newstead Abbey Park, 10 miles from where we had lived for the previous 13 years. Newstead Abbey is arguably the most desirable area in Nottinghamshire, and we were looking to design and build a dream house. Having anticipated that the sale of Park Lodge, our current house, would take a while, we were pleasantly proved wrong. The property sold in weeks, and for 15 months we lived in a delightful rented cottage only a mile from where we were building the new place.

Things were going pretty well at this time.

Our son, Nick, married, and for a time seemed happy with his spouse. Unfortunately this was not to last, and about ten years later they

FROM LITTLE ACORNS...

divorced. It is natural for a parent to be partisan, but I can truly say that although I don't like divorce, he had no option but to break away, and look to start again. The only good thing to result from this marriage was our first Granddaughter, Eve. I had seen my parents divorce, as had many of my friends, and I had nearly been there myself. I do hold the view that the continued undermining of the importance of the institution of marriage has in no small part contributed to the deterioration of society.

On the Synseal front, we were now occupying a 100,000 sq. ft. factory unit, and the original 15,000 ft place was rented to JBS, for them to continue the frame production activities they had purchased from me, just prior to Christmas. Our turnover was growing and we were introducing more extrusion lines and associated apparatus. It was decided that a further profit enhancing, independence-providing initiative was called for. This was a move further back up what we call 'the food chain'. The technical term is vertical integration. Instead of buying in the compound from which we produce the extruded profiles, we would set up a chemical blending facility. This was a huge job costing some £1,000,000, and taking over a year to install. As was now my mantra carved in stone, I needed to 'find my man to run this new operation'. The man was a qualified industrial chemist, called Vince Irving. In his early thirties, Vince fitted like a hand in a glove with the Synseal team. The site and plant were very impressive, and my new office was similarly so.

My personal knowledge had considerably increased with the growing of Synseal, and through the sale process of the fabrication arm, a really individual culture was constantly evolving. Synseal were rapidly becoming the force in the industry, but there was still a way to go. The next couple of years were a consolidation period, and this was an important ingredient in my skill set: knowing when to push ahead, and when to tidy up, as we nonchalantly referred to the process of consolidation. Our systems were upgraded and improved, our efficiency levels were under constant scrutiny, and the sales and marketing aspect was retained as a primary priority.

The ethos of the main men and, to an extent, the management as a whole, was one where the phrase "It can't be done" was outlawed. We prided ourselves on being quicker and better than the competition. There was no pomp and ceremony; I was addressed as Gary, or more often, just 'boss'. We had a laugh, but were as serious as a heart attack about Synseal. I introduced the kind of atmosphere where directors were

ANOTHER £1,000,000 INVESTMENT

'made men', a bit theatrical, and maybe even boyish, but the ambience was that of a team, in which we felt a responsibility for each other, and the idea of letting the team down was something not to be contemplated.

We instilled a methodology of investigating new opportunities and if considered viable, we would instigate, while others were still scratching their heads and procrastinating. We displayed an attitude of regarding the competition as a source of amusement. This was not arrogance, but confidence in our ability to get things done, and do them properly. An example of this creed was the unwritten policy whereby an idea for expansion or improvement would be given fair hearing, and the subsequent capex (Capital Expenditure) investment would be approved by me, provided that the return in gross profit would take no longer than 12 months. The guys knew this, and invariably it worked.

It is difficult to find one sentence to explain the fundamentals behind our success and the way we worked, but if I had to, I would probably say something like: quick, happy, good, and totally divorced from internal politics. If there was the slightest sign of an empire building scenario emerging, I/we would smash it down with alacrity and vengeance.

Although we were confident and displayed outward contempt for the competition, we would never become complacent. Our market intelligence became an integral part of the marketing facility. 'Soft targets' were the labels given to competitors who found themselves in difficulties of one kind or another. When we saw an opportunity to take advantage of what we called a 'soft target', we would devise the intended method of exploiting the situation, and implement it rapidly and aggressively. When I think back to my days of selling televisions, I now realise that I utilised similar tactics. I just did not know the actual terminology back in those days.

By the end of the nineties, Synseal was a major player in the extrusion industry, and as I stated earlier, we had improved and augmented our management team and infrastructure, so as not to trip up, as we grew.

By this time I had what I consider to be my 'A' team. When it came to the directors, I was now Chairman with very much hands-on executive duties; Malcolm was to become the best MD I could have wished for; Nick at the age of 29 was made sales and marketing director, and was improving by the day; Gareth Edwards was in charge of production; Vince Irving and big Rob Wilkinson ran operations. This gang was ultimately completed by the inclusion of Steve Musgrave, Robin Byron, and Brian Onions as FD. So, not far off my 'sevenths' rule. We had a good tier of senior managers: Jez Newton-Hewlett, Mark Robinson, Steve Scurrell, Dave (Bingo) Bingley, Dave Hughes and Jacky James. Nick recruited the best sales team possible, and we were the force to be reckoned with. There were many others, not the least of whom was my secretary for many years, Delma. One day I will find Delma making a mistake, maybe, but it hasn't happened in over 17 years.

Some of these people had been acquired using the Synseal recruitment method: when we wanted a person for a job, we would find the best guy for the particular position, through our contacts or market intelligence. Then we would simply make an offer they could not refuse. When asked why I adopted this method, I would say, "Because I can". In effect, I meant that while taking cognisance of individuals, the overriding consideration was the wellbeing of the company. Political correctness was as far from our considerations as it was possible to be. In my analogy between the military and business, there was me – the leader, with my two 4-star Generals, Malc and Nic; the other Generals – the directors, and the Colonels – the senior managers. I make no apologies for the repetition of my previous statement, that the most important resource is people. With good people, anything is possible; without them everything is virtually impossible.

Next came the times of more factories, new products, more revenues and profits, and one or two difficulties that came in the shape of being too successful. And then, the unions. •

TRIALS & TRIBULATIONS...

With the team working like a well-oiled machine, we were still heavily focused on our sales activity. Our marketing budget was significant, and we were gaining market share. By this time, we had more customers than any other profile/systems supplier. It had long been our policy to take a broad variety of clients. Investigations we carried out showed that no one type of client was necessarily better for us than another, so we took the big, the small, and those in between. The margins varied, but so did the exposure to credit risk, and servicing costs. As is always the case in the selling business, we were constantly seeking to improve the enquiry input in relation to the money expended.

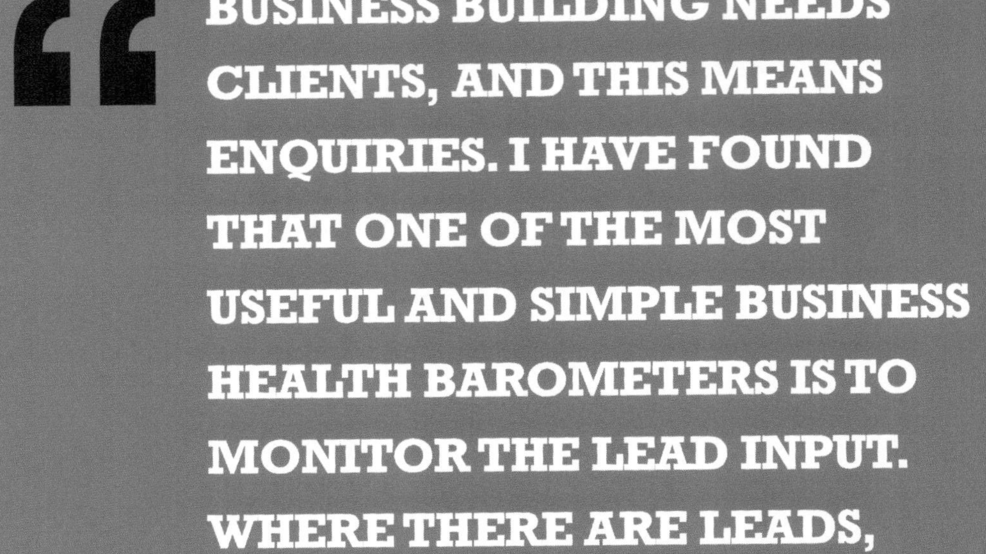

The old 1 in 3 conversion rate of leads to sales has been the Holy Grail in the sales world, and the Synseal guys were achieving this and better. Nick and I talked all the time about our progress, and how to become more efficient in our marketing. We had successfully branded our window systems: we had Contour, which was superseded by Shield, then eventually the Synergy range.

One of our best innovations did not produce what I believe it deserved: the Silhouette range.

The thought came to us that we actually manufactured our products by weight, but we sold them by the metre. The industry standard wall thickness for frame was 3 millimetres, therefore if we designed and produced a system with only 2 mill walls, it would virtually reduce the cost by one third. Given the fact that when fitted in a wall there would be absolutely no difference in appearance or performance, the fiscal advantages were huge. If our cost was £1 per kilo and a kilo was equivalent to 1 metre, and if we were then selling at £1.50 per metre, the sums are clear: the cost goes down to 70 pence per kilo/metre and we could sell at £1.35 per metre. Not only do we leave the competition trailing in our wake, but we actually increased profitability in both percentage and monetary terms.

Always be aware of the percentage/money trap. It is ok to say that your percentage has gone up, but if it is a percentage of a lower figure, then you have to sell more to cover your fixed costs, which is not always practical, due to various issues of investment, space and other resources.

I am reconciled to the fact that, had we invented the Silhouette system when the market was pre- trade buyer, that is to say, when it was still very much the home owner as direct customer, then I am certain we would have cleaned up. Now that our customers were the trade buyers, our competition managed to rubbish Silhouette by showing the rather gullible prospective clients that it was not as robust, due to its thinner wall sections. In reality this did not matter one jot, but nonetheless the competition did a good job of containing the damage that we intended to inflict upon them.

It is worth mentioning at this stage the cost of new manufacturing systems, which was considerable. Each new tool cost circa £70,000 and a whole suite, around three quarters of a million. Once when ordering a new suite, Malcolm discovered the unwritten rule that existed in the tool manufacturers' protocols: that the person ordering was given a 'reward' - basically a bribe. When Malcolm was offered this, he became incandescent; not only was it an affront to his personal integrity, but it also meant he had not screwed the supplier for the very best price, otherwise there would have been nothing left for the bribe. His reaction was verging on violence, as he dispatched the perpetrator with summary conviction.

Each year, the industry show is held at the NEC in Birmingham, and it was almost a prerequisite for all to exhibit there. A 'no show' would invite the competition to insinuate that you were not serious enough to display, and this would be very damaging to a company's reputation.

My handle on these shows was that they were never directly profitable in terms of enquiries to investment. I decided to change all that. The product, plastic extrusion, had increasingly become more of a commodity and as such Synseal was extremely price-conscious.

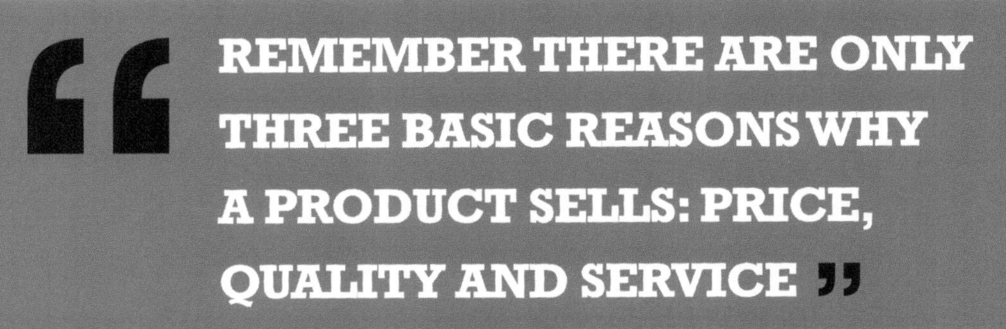

Synseal had the quality covered, and the service was as good as anyone's. Therefore, given a price benefit, the sales would grow. In order to achieve this objective, it was necessary to ensure that the whole company was tight. The cost base had to be perfect, and the operation lean and mean. Too many firms at the NEC would treat the show as a PR stunt and a 4-day piss up.

Their stands were big and expensive, but in my view they did little to generate real business. We were at the stage where we could maintain good profits and sell our products at £1.65 per metre. When set against the industry average of over £2, it does not take a genius to see what a market advantage this would give us.

I headed up one show personally. I had a vision of how it would work, and wanted every detail precisely as I visualised. I did, however, bend to one area of opinion: this was to use printed posters on the exhibition stand instead of the Day-Glo fluorescent paper with felt tip penned messages. You probably now get the flavour of where my head was: I wanted to create a very simple and inexpensive stand, which told a straightforward but powerful message. The message was: "From £1.65 Per Metre." There was no expensive stand building, just the delivery stillages, full of profile. These were arranged to form a sort of enclosure.

I instructed the staff on the stand to leave their suits at home, and they all dressed in smart blue v neck sweaters and dark grey trousers. Again, this was very different from the norm, and friendlier to the audience. My details extended to banning booze from the stand, but insisting that we served tea and coffee, very hot. This ploy was based on the anticipation that once having been given something, most people don't leave until they have shown the courtesy of finishing their drink. This worked, and when the stand became very busy, it was useful to hold people there until there was a Synseal sales person available, to do the business. To this day, we hold the record for one of the most cost effective stands the Glassex exhibition has ever produced. In contrast with the cost of the average stand – about 100k – the total cost of this production was under 20k and it produced some 150 good enquiries. The usual lead generation for a stand was around 20. After the guys converted over 50 of these leads within a short period, we were very proud of our revolutionary concept. Needless to say we were not popular with the other stand occupants, but this was pleasing, as we intended to be disliked and feared by our competitors. I was told that one serious extrusion company owner told another that, "Dutton is destroying the margins and lowering the quality of the show!"

I could not have been more delighted.

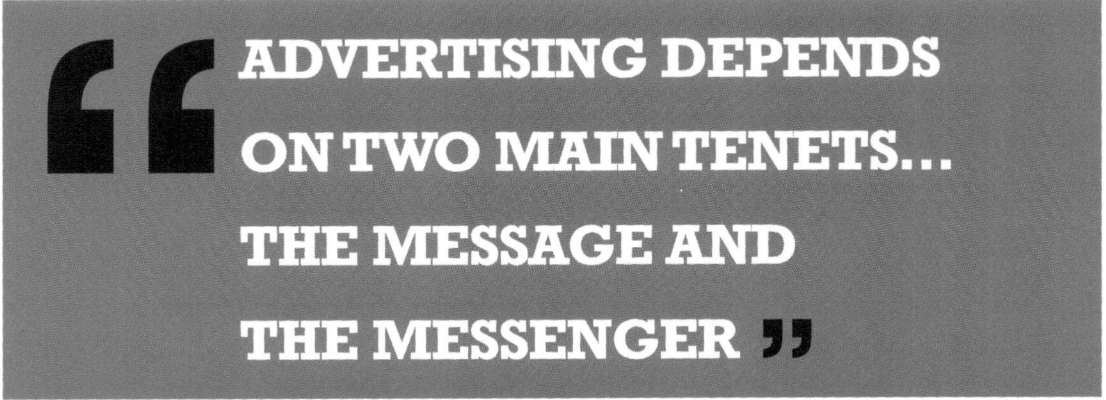

Get a powerful message and use a powerful medium to deliver it.

One problem appeared, and we used it to our advantage. As I said earlier, we had a big customer base and we needed to keep up our conversion rate from leads to sales. We arrived at the point where we were becoming hoisted by our own petard. With clients covering the length and breadth of the country, we were receiving new enquiries and having to decline to supply half of them; because of the proximity of our existing trade clients to the area of operation of the new trade enquirer. Had we taken on a new client to compete with them, then we ran the risk of the existing client spitting out his dummy and moving his allegiance to another extruder; clearly not a good way to run our business.

At the time, our average order value was in the region of £1800. The new plan was to sell additional products into the existing customer base. Nothing was left unconsidered, from gaskets to work boots, from patios to glass units. The appeal to the client was clear, he could reduce the number of suppliers and have more goods delivered on one truck. From a marketing point of view it was a piece of cake. The clients we had were simply told, "Just try this gasket and if you like it we will supply at a preferential price."

We were shooting fish in a barrel, so to speak. Later, I was quoted in the FT using this expression to describe taking customers from some competitors. Perhaps a more professional description would be 'selling to a receptive audience,' but you get the drift, I am sure.

In the next chapter I tell how we began to roll out more products into the customer base, in a fashion that would ultimately double our turnover in the early noughties.

Before that, however, we did experience another obstacle. The bloody unions.

Synseal was one of the largest private employers in our district, so naturally the scourge that is the unions decided we should be infected with their involvement. Whispers started, concerning the fact that we had members of staff who had designs on the company becoming unionised. There are always some people who think they can have their two minutes of glory by being militant.

Before we knew where we were, we had union types standing outside the factory gates trying to seduce our workers with overtures of all sorts of rubbish. It escalated apace, and very soon there was nearly enough support to make the prospect of union intrusion a reality. This resulted in the only occasion in which I found myself in a minority of one. Even my MD and friend Malcolm broached the subject of me holding a dialogue with these clowns.

I very vociferously said, "No way! I will close the company before I agree to let them over the doorstep!"

Understandably, my people were worried at the magnitude of my stance, my wife included. Having shown teeth, I had to follow through.

I was interviewed and appeared on the main TV news programmes, even being referred to as the new Eddy Shah, of the union bashing in the Thatcher era of the '80s.

I acquired the support of some friends in politics (profoundly right-leaning friends) and spoke with our local MP, Geoff Hoon.

Geoff was a cabinet minister for the Labour party and he showed no sympathy for my cause in keeping the unions at bay. Geoff and I had a

THE RT. HON. G.HOON MP OFFICIATING AT NEW FACTORY OPENING

fairly difficult relationship for some time, with me generally berating him on a weekly local radio show I worked on for a couple of years. In later times, Geoff was helpful to Synseal and even officiated in the opening of our next factory. Then we were one of the largest private employers in his constituency.

The union movement had adopted a rather hypocritical policy of non-confrontation at the time, and this where I saw my edge. It worked. A well-known media interviewer I had spoken with called me from the annual meeting of the TUC where the main attacking union, along with all the other splinter unions, were present. My source informed me in a very clandestine tone that all in attendance were given a clipping of information regarding the battle with Synseal. Much to the annoyance of the unions involved, the TUC told them to leave Synseal alone. The explanation was that they were not sure if Dutton was bluffing in his statement intending to close the company if unionisation came in, but they could not afford to take the chance. Hundreds of workers being made unemployed and me blaming the unions would fly in the face of the union movement trying to show a more placatory face.

I had won. The proverbial burglar was frightened by my protection technique and they went somewhere else to do their damage. I am still asked if I would have really closed my company. Only I truly know, but the answer is "Yes." I would have done so.

In modern times of employment law, unions are an anachronism. Their record goes before them. They have been responsible for the demise of many industries. They are the antithesis of their stated aims to support the worker. They are the prime movers in thousands becoming unemployed. When a crowd of people set out to inflict their views on others, they are called bullies.

Synseal has always been proud of its firm and fair dealings with employees. At the end of the day, a business is only as good as the people working within it. If the staff exercise the ultimate sanction available to them: they can withdraw their labour, and then there is no business. •

THE BIG MOVE

As Synseal grew, we needed more and more space. Cash was no longer a major issue, since we were very profitable and cash generative. In the past, I had set up a SSAS (Small Self-Administered Pension). I used this to purchase the second factory we occupied, before selling the window fabrication to JBS. The benefit of this type of scheme was that not only was it a pension for the future but also had attractive tax-efficient aspects. After leasing this factory to JBS for a number of years, they eventually vacated and I had it back in my possession. It was no longer much use to me for the expanding extrusion operation. It had seemed huge a decade previously, but now, at 15000 sq feet, it was no longer seen in the same light. Nowadays our space requirements were on a scale of ten to twenty times larger. I will explain shortly how we utilised this unit to our advantage.

I had created a small group of companies in order to provide for various contingencies: retaining flexibility for future opportunities, whilst leaving my growing property portfolio as a separate stand-alone business. The holding company, Synseal Holdings Limited (SHL), owned the factories, and rented them to the operating company at an arm's length, commercial rate. SHL was also the company into which I transferred profits from Synseal Extrusions Ltd (SEL) by way of dividends or loans.

> **“TAKE SPARE CASH OUT OF TRADING COMPANIES. I BELIEVE THIS KEEPS THE MANAGEMENT ON THEIR TOES WHEN COLLECTING DEBTS”**

One deal involved looking to buy a big unit, for more space, next door to our current location.

> **“MAINTAIN THE HEAD QUARTERS ON ONE SITE. SATELLITE OFFICES COST MORE IN MANAGEMENT, AND ARE MORE DIFFICULT TO CONTROL”**

This new unit was on offer through an agent, at £4,200,000. The cash was in the Synseal Holdings account, but the estate agents were, as I have come to expect, their usual dilatory selves. The vendor was a large public group, and the main man there was Sir Harry. After months of being messed around by what I considered fairly feckless estate agents, I faxed Sir Harry, telling him bluntly that his appointed agents were wasting time, and that if he really wanted to sell the factory, then he had until noon on the following Monday. Otherwise I would rescind my interest entirely. I have used this type of ultimatum many times to best advantage.

9.15am on Monday, my secretary called me and said Sir Harry had telephoned. I left returning the call for a posturing period of an hour. I rang Sir Harry, and after the normal niceties, Harry asked, "Do you have the cash?"

With as much effrontery as I could muster, I told him in no uncertain terms that his agent had known for months that more than sufficient cash was sitting in the bank to facilitate the purchase. Having now reached the point where I could retain a position as master of the situation, I told Harry that if we now had a deal, then he must fax me his confirmation within one hour.

Being a good operator, he responded: "Why don't you push me? You will have it within thirty minutes!"

Twelve minutes later it arrived: done deal!

Agents of all varieties have always appeared to be fairly mediocre business people, to me. I may be overdoing it, but they often come across as thinking their opinion is the only one that matters, and to me as a professional salesman, I see this attitude as wrong. Just because one person's favorite colour is red, it doesn't mean that others will think so too. Over the years, I was propositioned many times by advertising agents. I never recall doing business with any, but I did develop a method of having a bit of fun with them. Say their pitch was based on something like providing me with 1000 enquiries, at a cost of £20,000.

I would say, "Ok, so you are sure that if I give you 20k, you will provide me with 1000 leads?"

"Definitely, sir!" came the response, "Without doubt - at least!"

"Fine," said I, "but I tell you what... I will give you – not 20k, but 25k – providing you get me at least 800 enquiries."

The look of incredulity on their faces was wonderful. This guy was offering to pay more for less than they had pitched!

Then I would drop the bomb, "But if I don't get at least the 800, you get nothing."

Never, ever, did an ad agent take me up on this deal.

Back with the serious matter of business building, and using the old 'spare' factory unit. The project of increasing our revenues, by supplying more product types into the customer base, worked well. The average order value was up from £1800 to £2500. We called these 'added value products', which is not strictly the correct phrase, but it was the description we used. The next added value product was to be the big one.

Conservatories would shove the average order value to over £4000, and become 50% of the Synseal turnover.

The major players in uPVC conservatories had been been established companies. The profits of some of these firms were well above what was the norm in the general market. Upon investigation it was discovered that the lack of serious competition allowed this situation to exist. The explanation was in part the I.P. (patents) that had been taken out by the players in the market.

The competition's tactic of swatting all comers with their big cheque book and big lawyers was not going to work with Synseal. We were too big and ballsy to be frightened off. Our strategy was to investigate the patents very carefully, and then to produce a conservatory range which was not only better and cheaper, but did not contravene any I.P. This is where the old empty factory came into use. Our plan was to obtain samples of all the competition's ranges of conservatories, and having designed our own, we would then proceed to test the all the competition's types, as well as our own, to destruction. Over the next six months, we had achieved this goal, and were satisfied that our patent attorneys, Forrester Kettley, had made certain that our designs were not in breach of any competitors' patents.

With our increasingly sophisticated market intelligence methods, we were fully aware of the response of the competition to our entry into the conservatory game. I believe that the general attitude to our move into conservatories was one of arrogance, regarding Synseal as incapable of making any serious inroads into a market that had hitherto been serviced by a few companies only. This was a major mistake, but they had been allowed to become fat in commercial terms, and did not recognise the threat we presented until it was too late for them to defend their position with any seriousness.

I have long held the view that the best way to deal with a bully is to hit him. Firstly, they don't expect it, and secondly, when it happens they often don't know what to do about it. This was my tactic with the competition, and then we actually had the temerity to challenge the validity of some I.P. held by certain competitors

It would never have been possible for any of the competition to block our attack completely, but they could have slowed us down had they not been so complacent. Had I been them, I would have rounded up my team and used a metaphorical approach, something like: "We have to put the vintage Dom Perignon back in the fridge and make do with the Moët."

In effect Synseal did what Synseal do, and that was to attack where we saw opportunity and take market share from the rest of the competition.

We were flying. Profits were over £1,000,000 per month, and things were going well. Then, one Sunday lunchtime one of my 'made men' – Vince – crashed his car and was killed. My team were devastated, me included. How could this have happened to one of our boys? Looking back, I realise now that for the best part of a year, we were effectively grieving. The whole atmosphere was one of sadness and depression.

There is a tree planted in the Synseal grounds with a plaque reading: "Vince Irving, a real Synseal man."•

I COULD HAVE BEEN A BILLIONAIRE

During the first few years of the new millennium, M and A (Mergers and Acquisitions) activity was high; there was plenty of cash swimming round the markets, and with Synseal now holding the position of market leader in its sub-sector, the offers started to come from various sources to buy the company. We were making stellar profits, and one year achieved an EBIT (Earnings Before Interest and Tax) of over £14,000,000. Not only were we profitable, but our ratios also made Synseal attractive to predators. Since the very early times, I had ensured that we focused on maximising our profitability in percentage terms as well as monetary.

I have always retained a degree of skepticism when reading accounts of companies with huge revenues, and then only 2 or 3 percent ROS (Return On Sales). In my view, it is possible, with a little financial massaging or even simple arithmetical shortcomings in the audit process, for the results to lack complete integrity.

Ok, we all know the margins obtained by the 'stack it high, sell it cheap' ethos of the supermarket retailers are reliable, but when it comes to manufacturing industries, there are far too many variables in the mix to be totally confident that the profits are really as stated. I like decent strides of profit margins, and my target was permanently to be in double digits or better in terms of percentages. Usually I was reluctant to sanction a new budget if I could not see net profits in the teens of percentage. The concept of being a bust fool has never appealed to me.

> **“TURNOVER IS VANITY; PROFIT IS SANITY”**

Later, I will describe some fundamentals of looking to sell or buy a business. It goes without saying that there are many elements that go into a profitable business, whilst retaining a very competitive price to the customer.

In my 30 years with Synseal, I confess to never having quite achieved one of my goals, which was to show overheads at 20% of turnover or less. I think we got down to 21% one year. By way of comparison, the average in my industry was over 30%, so it becomes clear how we achieved both very competitive prices to customers, and produced good profits. The economies of scale often help profitability in terms of cost base to turnover. It is always worth remembering the fact that reduction in overheads ratio does not mean reduction in costs, for the sake of cost reduction.

My MD Malcolm has long preached to his people that the better way is to increase efficiency: same meat, different veg, so to speak. We see all too often, with huge organisations and with governments, that they enjoy economies of scale, but then find themselves having to savage costs through closures and consequential redundancies, after any period of adversity. If they had been on top of the job, and more proactive, the damage could sometimes have been limited.

I have some thoughts that the very concept of the PLC scenario is a little flawed, in straightforward business management terms. When one thinks of a new enterprise: the knowledge base, diligence and specific skills sets that go into getting things off the ground, it becomes realistic to consider my point. When a business grows and floats, diversifies and integrates, and moves into areas which are further away from the core skill set that existed in the early days, the chances of problems increase. I accept that companies can buy talent. I have done so, and I accept that the levels of commercial knowledge will increase. My point is that with growth, the whole operation becomes more unwieldy, with a reduced attention to detail. In the PLC situation, there is a constant requirement for both income and / or share price enhancement. OK, if one company buys another at preferable P.E. level, then things should improve. However in needing to prioritise this never-ending quest to keep their market stock appeal, the company can drift further and further from its core expertise. They go into conglomerate integration and into markets not as well understood as their original. In this process of growth, an accompanying danger can develop, whereby the dilution of understanding and 'finger on the pulse management' results in what the City refers to as 'corrections' being necessitated. I regard this expression as a euphemism for the escalation of knowledge drift, which needs 'correcting'.

Maybe an over simplification, but not, I suggest, totally without merit. How many times do we hear a PLC Chairman announcing at the AGM that the wellbeing of the company will improve when he brings in a new Sales Director or whoever? The shareholders go along with this process, repeatedly, until the credibility of the announcements becomes exhausted. Then the Chairman falls on his sword, before suffering the ignominy of being pushed. Cynical I may be, but I do believe that top public company executives are often better at keeping their jobs than they are at doing them.

To complete my point, I cannot leave the politicians without a mention. These people are likely to have never had a 'proper job,' let alone been equipped to run Great Britain PLC. It would be unfair to say that they are all the same, but for sure, I have asked many a politician to adopt a policy containing three primary elements:

1. **Answer a straight question, with a straight answer.**
2. **Do your job. Do not just keep your job.**
3. **Stop bringing my country into disrepute.**

I have long since enjoyed the big London shows: Phantom, Les Miserables and others. However, one of the very best shows in town, running for many years, is Prime Minister's Question Time. Showing every week, it is brilliant, with a recognisable cast, a great plot, and wonderful oratory.

The problem occurred to me after walking out of one session I'd just watched. I experienced a sensation of despair. This is not a show. These are the people we pay to run our country. If kids in a playground performed like them, we would give them a thick ear (EU permitting, of course).

I have, over the years, been a serious contributor to the Tory party funds. A few years ago my contribution was £50,000, which I discovered was sufficient to allow me 'direct access'. This is not literal, but it does mean that I can get my point across to the party leader occasionally. The leader at the time was Right Honourable Michael Howard. I did consider that he stood a good chance of getting the Conservatives back into power, but unfortunately he failed. Michael is an intelligent and committed man, with many sound principles; he was also a 'big beast', a grown-up in a world where many fresh-faced MPs would not have looked out of place carrying a satchel instead of a brief case.

Many times have I been invited to Conservative party get-togethers; one of these occasions was to have lunch with David Cameron and about 15 other local business people. David was then leader of the party, and arrived at this low key event, demonstrating his quiet charisma and amiable persona. I was seated next to him at lunch, and in conversation he asked a question that in a more public forum would have been absolutely taboo.

"What would you have us do when we get into power, Gary?"

I thought all my birthdays had come at once! This opportunity alone must be worth my 50K contribution, so I replied: "Three things. Stop immigration dead in its tracks, outlaw more political correctness being inflicted upon us, and thirdly – come out of the EU and let's get back to the common market concept."

There was a general, "Hear, hear!" from those assembled.

Sadly, the only one who did not appear to hear was David himself. His retort to me was to the effect of: "But we can't reverse these things."

"Well, what's the point of getting you elected if you can't influence these areas of concern to many of the citizens?" methinks.

As mentioned at the outset of this book, politically, I am of a right-leaning tendency. I don't want to support less fortunate people who don't want to work. I do completely support the unfortunate people who genuinely can't work. Coming from a council estate, and with no qualifications, I do not consider that I am any more fortunate than the next man. I just tried harder and never gave up. Having a social conscience is something I pride myself in, as I will hopefully evidence later in this book. When I heard Gordon Brown saying that the fortunate should pay a little more, I could have gladly hit him. Does he not have the sense to realise that 40% of a lot is already more than 25% of a far smaller amount? Furthermore, an extra 10% on a higher rate tax is 25% increase. Does he think we are all stupid? Thank goodness we got rid of him before he took the country into total economic meltdown. The hypocrite was the prime mover in allowing the UK banks to run riot a few years ago. He and his predecessor have an awful lot to answer for, but I don't suppose they ever will.

I learned an expression a long time ago which I strongly subscribe to::

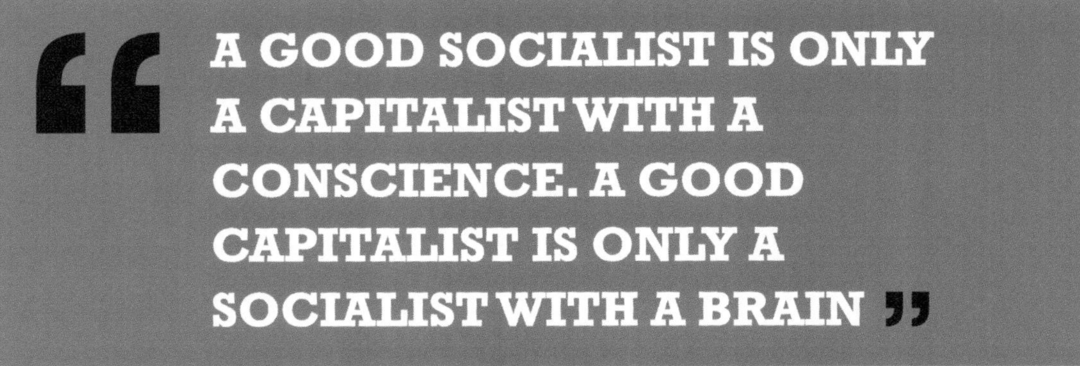

That just about sums it up for me.

Back to Synseal becoming the target for several unsolicited approaches for me to sell. After selling Synseal Fabrications I received a bid for £12M for Synseal Extrusions, followed by a bid from multi-million dollar American outfit called Masco. This proposition was interesting, and had me thinking for a while. Masco were a very amenable team, and had a very straightforward approach and criteria. I liked them, and could see myself being in harmony with their culture. The Masco style was that if the target passed the three tests of: having £50M revenues or over; ROS (Return On Sales) in the teens of percent, and being well managed, then they did not go in for the usual level of bullshit. They did not need to. They were a cash buyer, knew what they were doing, and had no reason to use banks for funding. Funders were, of course, overly fastidious in their approach, some of which was necessary, and some of it simple back-watching. In discussions with Masco, I asked how much time they would want to have their bean counters spend on due diligence. Five days, was the response, against the accepted minimum of five weeks, which made Masco appear very much my sort of company.

Over the next weeks, I spoke with a number of my advisers, and notwithstanding my wife's appeals for me to accept the offer, I declined. There were two primary reasons for my rejection: firstly, I was confident that Synseal would soon be far more valuable, and the second reason I cannot overstress: the thought process was agonising. 'Agony' is the only word strong enough to describe the feeling. I had not yet arrived at the point at which I wanted to sell my baby, no matter what the price. And even more importantly, I had no plan for Gary after Synseal. Big chunks of change can be very enticing, and some might think that you

can do whatever you want afterwards, but I am a businessman, and if I sold, there would be no serious business for me to run the day after the sell deal was done.

This situation will not apply to everyone given the option to sell, but I have seen many guys exit and regret later.

I should mention that I was turning down £27M, which may sound somewhat greedy, but I don't believe this to be the case. In my aspiration to be a good businessman, I consider it my responsibility to try to do the best deals possible. An athlete does not start the race with the intention of coming second.

In terms of our personal lifestyle issues, Carol and I were now living quite expensively; not the least of our extravagances was the purchase of a share of a private jet though the Net Jets shared ownership deal. I had looked at buying my own jet, but decided that the Net Jets proposal suited me best. I did not want what would have been another job of

work, if I had bought a plane. Net Jets is like owning a piece of a taxi, and having the use of a taxi service. After 9/11 the thought of going through airports, with all the distasteful aspects that grew to be part of the experience, was abhorrent to me.

We now had a new boat in the Med, as well as a new river barge in the UK inland waterways. I do like extravagance, but not waste. By my reckoning, once you have twenty million net worth, your lifestyle does not change much, up to having 50M. Over that level, things can alter exponentially.

Maybe I could have been a billionaire had I been prepared to put everything on the line. Having started out with nothing, I had nothing to lose in the early days. The situation changed and the thought of risking everything was one I could not entertain. Many times, we looked at the possibility of augmenting the Synseal growth via acquisition. If this was to become part of our strategy, the buying of big companies would involve using the City, with investment banks providing much of the acquisition funding. When getting into bed with these institutions, not unsurprisingly, they want to cover their backs, by ensuring that the person they are backing is fully committed in every sense.

Once, when negotiating with a venture capital company, I offered to put up ten million of my own money to facilitate a purchase. This was not enough for them. They wanted me, belt, braces and a piece of string. In essence, they wanted Synseal to be at risk, and this was not on my agenda. Banks are ok when things are going well, but don't ever forget that when the going gets tough, they will bury a borrower without the slightest compunction. If ever this view needed vindication, the period from 2007 to date does the job perfectly. Banks have sent countless businesses down that could have survived, given a little help from them. The banks themselves received help from us, the UK tax payer.

I may never be a billionaire, but I can happily live with that. Just by way of a side comment, we find these days that the word 'billion' appears ever more frequently in our vocabulary. Sometimes I think people are not fully conversant with the enormity of the difference between a million and a billion. The best way I can make the distinction is as follows:

“CONVERT A MILLION INTO SECONDS OF TIME, THEN CONVERT A BILLION INTO SECONDS OF TIME; ONE MILLION SECONDS IS JUST SHORT OF 12 DAYS, ONE BILLION SECONDS IS 32 YEARS!”

OUR HOME
FROM 1997

ACQUISITION

When Carol and I were holidaying on our 85 foot boat in Italy, I received a call from one Greg Hutchins, of Lupus Capital, a quoted PLC shell company he had acquired for the purpose of creating a new Tompkins type group. Greg had spent 20 years with Tompkins, James Hanson, and Gordon White, building one of the most successful conglomerate investment vehicles. The nickname for this outfit was 'Guns and Buns', derived from its ownership of Smith and Wesson gun makers, and Mr Kipling pies.

Greg had disagreed with the City in the late '90s, by refusing to become an investor in the dot com bubble. I share Greg's view, to the extent that conventional business sense can't come to terms with the concept of valuing a loss-making company. More recently, I have learned that the 'new' City method is through multiples of revenues, which I still struggle to understand; but then, who am I? A lot of people who have never made profit in their lives have sold for squillions. I remember hearing of one dot com executive telling the City that the company had 'regularised its losses', whatever that means.

Greg is a very persuasive fellow, and he flew to visit with me on my boat, trying his damnedest to get me to agree to a deal to sell Synseal.

The offer was outstanding, but I had now developed the attitude of not putting myself through the agony process, so I told him no. I did help him in a small way with another acquisition he made, which interestingly led on to my strategy for eventually disposing of Synseal. That occasion was, however, still some five years away.

In the meantime, we were looking to grow the beast that was now Synseal, and if I am honest, I was in a position to indulge my appetite for learning more. Although we had been involved in the sale and acquisition process, in both a direct and peripheral fashion, I knew that SEL (Synseal Extrusions Ltd) needed to make a quantum move and buy another business that had its own product identity. We needed to bolt on another product range, with its own customer base, which was loyal to that particular brand.

It is at this stage that I must explain that the original storyline has been completely revised on the advice of my lawyers. I find it very frustrating to completely omit specific references, but that's the world we live in. I will relate in a more generic fashion how this important part of the Synseal development took place. Having identified a suitable business that was to be disposed of by the current shareholders, a deal was agreed and completed at an eight figure price. The business produced a range of products which were fairly well regarded in the market but did not fit well within the strategic objectives of the vendor group.

The advantages to SEL were significant, and following the usual legal process, Malc, my corporate lawyer Mr. Gavin Cummings and I were feeling pleased with our purchase. The relocation of some of the business's activities to our headquarters was dealt with in a swift and efficient manner by big Rob Wilkinson, Gareth Edwards and their crew. Indeed, it was necessary for me to rent additional storage capacity in order to facilitate the additional stock until such time as the extra 100,000 sq ft of factory space presently in build was completed.

It has been my view that whenever a business is purchased there is likely to be a variety of "unknowns" which only appear post deal.

On this occasion there were a number of these, some of which entailed making decisions to discontinue a number of the products due to poor tooling condition, the replacement of which would have involved a six months for new tool manufacture, during which time the customer base for the products might have evaporated. The risk was deemed as too high in my terms of being a risk manager therefore we chose to concentrate on integrating into our existing product range only some of the new profiles systems. I now move on from this particular event, but suffice to say that there are a number of lessons learned listed in summary in the later chapters .... Interlude, and a Few For the Road.

Looking back, there are no regrets with the decision to buy this business and it did facilitate and complement our position. The eventual payback in terms of gross profit contribution against final price paid was approximately one year.

The best advice I can offer when becoming an acquisitor is: do your own due diligence and make sure it is very thorough. There are occasions when even individuals and organizations such as myself and Synseal must look to developing the enterprise by acquisition, but I remain an organic builder first, and acquirer very much second. Post acquisition tidying up can be very expensive and time consuming. Further investment is often required in order to maximize return on the price paid. There must always remain a strong focus on any closure costs that may ensue. These can take many forms, but redundancies and commitment to leases regularly feature.

By way of a personal note, during this time my beloved younger brother Stewart had fallen very ill. The eventual diagnosis was that he had a brain tumour. Stew passed away on the 21st August 2006.

In preparation for this book, I had imagined that telling about this event in my life would somehow help with the grief which I still feel. In practice, I can't describe the desolation and misery that still comes over me, so I will simply say I still miss him, and always will. •

SEEKING NEW HORIZONS

The years 2006 and 2007 were interesting and varied in activity, and on a personal level I had two particular objectives. One of these was seeking some guidance on the best time for me to move towards the exit from Synseal. I knew from past experience that unless the conditions were right, then I would not be comfortable with such a major change. For sure, I would never sell until I was sure that there was 'life after Synseal', and that meant a trading business to go to. Investment businesses are ok, but it's not like a real job.

The decision was to discover a product upon which we could build the Synseal successor. During 2006, some of my guys introduced me to a product which immediately struck me as the answer: composite doors.

My plan was to build a smaller business with more of a 'lifestyle' dimension, which would leave me working with some of the colleagues who had come to be important in my life.

I have met many interesting people through my business career, and in my shooting and boating activities.

Having constantly had the urge to learn, I chose to use a few of these contacts in order to try and get a handle on how other people had exited their previous heavy duty careers. The first was General Sir

Michael Wilkes, an extremely distinguished military man. Having had the pleasure of game shooting with this big guy (big in just about every sense of the word), I took the opportunity to ask him one day what it was like for him when he stepped down from being one of the country's most accomplished military generals. His answer was fairly nonchalant, as befits a man of his stature.

He said, "Well, when the army had finished with me, they made me Governor of Jersey, so I just moved on to another career."

The salient point was the part about the army having finished with him. This explanation gained more reason when I asked the same question of Admiral Rory McLean. He is an extremely charismatic guy, and at one time was responsible for HMS Invincible. Again, Rory's time in the service of his country was exemplary. He told me that in the military it is not a question of when the individual wishes to leave his position. It does not matter if the person concerned is ready to change.

"When the MOD decides that you are finished in an operational capacity, that's it. You get a desk in Westminster, and perhaps a promotion in rank. So you see, Gary, we guys do not have the luxury of our destiny being in our own hands, as you business types have."

Basically the same answer as the General.

Next I spoke with Sir Harry, from whom I had bought a factory some years previously. Being from the commercial world, Harry had more identification with my situation than the others. His advice was not definitive but nonetheless satisfactory for my purposes: "You will know when you are ready. Just as you have known when and how to build your company."

CLAY SHOOTING

With this insight, and with composite doors identified as the new generation of domestic entrance, I knew where I was going. There would be a job after SEL, so the usual research and preparatory work was to commence.

Synseal was on target for a £100,000,000 turnover, and I was increasingly adopting the role of Chairman. Over and above the orthodox duties that chairmen undertake, I described my job as a cross between a politician and a referee. I was semi-redundant, until there was a development or a crisis.

As you might imagine, in a fast company like Synseal, there were inevitable problems that I had to resolve, and there was a constant theme of development that ran through the very genes of Synseal. We were very busy, but the team were as good as they get, and with Malc and Nick becoming better by the day, there was rarely a situation which remotely fazed us.

Money was no longer an issue; the banks were now holding our money, not lending us theirs. I got it into my head that I wanted to pay myself a huge dividend and have a very big chunk in my own personal accounts. The actual reason was not particularly rational, but I did it; probably because I could.

Now confident that the market for composite doors was the next product to be involved in, through channels we found a company called Thermo Tru, owned by an American parent, and working out of South Wales. This company were manufacturers of composite doors, and owing to poor policy-making within Thermo Tru, and consequential losses, the American overlords had determined that the UK operation was to close. With our methodology well-honed, off we went, and very soon had bought the assets of Thermo Tru, along with recruiting some hand-picked and specialist staff members.

As with our past history, the meticulous process of spending months fine-tuning all aspects of this intended new project was underway. My intention was to start Door-Stop International as a totally separate company, and the necessary infrastructure arrangements had to be provided. The first objective was to find suitable premises. I took the opportunity to take on a newly built 100,000 sq foot factory, complete with good offices, from a developer with whom I had dealt when creating the 500,000 foot, five factory Synseal site. The deal was a rental, with an option to buy at a later date.

I have found option agreements a very useful facility as they allow for flexibility in developing projects without the encumbrance of total commitment. If the project is aborted, then the long-term problems can be mitigated when using this tactic. As an added bonus, the unit was next door to the Synseal site: there was only a fence between the two. This not only made the logistics of management for research more workable, but somewhere in the back of my mind, something was telling me that this would one day prove a clever move.

A couple of defining events happened in 2007, in respect of the future. The first of these was my decision to consummate my intention of eventual departure from Synseal, and the second was the economic crash.

The 'consummation of intention to exit', as I called it, was by way of a very extravagant four day holiday thrown for all my directors and their spouses, along with selected members of the senior management, during which I would announce my intentions.

I chartered the Christina O motor yacht, which I had previously visited with my wife. The gig was about as upmarket as I could make it. Christina O is 325 feet long, and was once owned by the late Aristotle Onassis. She has been totally renovated, but still retained the ambiance of a previous era and her glorious past. On board was the feeling of history, with pictures of John and Jackie Kennedy, Maria Callas, Winston Churchill, Frank Sinatra, and countless other A-Listers of yesteryear. The swimming pool on the aft deck was spectacular with its original mosaic tiling, and polished brass surround. It had the added benefit of being hydraulically powered, so that it converted to a dance floor when raised. There is a photograph of Churchill and Onassis sitting in deck chairs, with the pool floor lowered, but not flooded for swimming. Apparently this was to allow the old guys to

be in the open air with their cigars, without being buffeted by the wind when the ship was under way.

The reasons I used a yacht were simple: because I felt at home on the water, anyway, it was the height of luxury. The food, booze and the whole thing was magnificent and very expensive. All 26 of my guests congregated in formal attire for the first evening's Gala Dinner in the fabulous saloon. At the appropriate time, I asked for attention and after paying some heartfelt compliments to my people, I gently announced that in the not too distant future, I would be looking to withdraw from Synseal on a full time basis. I chose my words carefully, so as not to be too astounding, which might have given rise to concerns in those present. As it turned out, they all understood, and were very supportive of my position. I did explain that I would reciprocate their loyalty and do everything in my power to ensure that the team were not disadvantaged

MY GREAT TEAM ON THE MOTOR YACHT CHRISTINA O

when the time came for me to step aside. Of interest, at this time, I calculated that I had an accumulated total of over 100 years' working with the 8 'made men' present.

Having made my intentions public, we continued to enjoy the 4 days and 3 nights cruising the French and Italian coast, finishing off with the ship anchored in the bay of St Tropez. The final night was the pièce de résistance. For many years, I had known a rock band based in France, and the sax player, Phil, had become a good friend of mine. The band came on board, and gave us all one of the best nights imaginable. My guests returned home, while Carol and I embarked on our own yacht, and headed for the Islands off shore for a couple of days' R and R.

Then came the economic disaster, which I fortunately realised was going to be like no other experienced since the Second World War. It was my job to deal with crisis situations, and hopefully turn adversity into opportunity. Be sure of one thing, despite the politicians constantly asserting that the event took place in 2008, it was, as sure as shit, well established in 2007. It just manifested thereafter. The perfect storm ensued, with stagflation and banks effectively closed for business, all at the same time. In the past, we had often benefited from recessionary periods. In September 1992, the UK was ignominiously booted out of the ERM, and others were bemoaning the fact that with Sterling devalued, business would become very difficult. This was the case for companies which did not have sufficient flexibility, but for Synseal it was a grand opportunity. The dross element within the competition went to the wall, and we grabbed market share with both hands. In 2007 however, it would be different, and turning adversity into opportunity would not be so simple.

By way of a footnote to this chapter, I mention that I had committed myself to studying and taking additional exams in order to become a qualified Yacht Master. The process was time consuming, and attaining the license to be a rated Yacht Captain was far from easy.

On reflection, I was probably influenced in taking on this additional project, by the terrible loss of Brother Stewart. Maybe it helped distract my thoughts, and help with the grief I was suffering.

Next comes: me using the "D" word, frantically spending £20,000,000 in four days, and being awarded the MBE. •

THE CRASH AND DOOR STOP OPENS FOR BUSINESS

There was a feeling of anticipation rather than trepidation existing throughout Synseal during the summer of 2007. The guys were doing their stuff as always, and I decided where and how I was heading next. The announcement of my looking to take my leave of Synseal had been made, and 'life after Synseal', in terms of my career, was fairly well established. Composite doors were to be the vehicle through which I would head up the new company, Door-Stop International, and the factory premises were secured.

The tooling bought from the defunct company Thermo Tru for the venture was now in house, and the research into developing a basic business plan was being addressed.

Also on the 'jobs to do list' was to explore the sale of Synseal process, and all that goes with such a strategic move. I have more than once indicated my view that people are the resource of utmost importance within any organisation, and in the autumn of 2007 the most perverse of events took place. The economic crash was my chance to turn adversity into an opportunity. More on this, shortly.

The DSI (Door Stop International) plan was coming together, and it was intended that my son Nick would be the first main man to move over to the

new company. He was, along with me, the guy with the sales and marketing skills, and as with any new venture, getting sales moving is numero uno in order of importance. No sales, and there's nothing for the rest of the firm to do. Not only was it necessary to have someone focused on the DSI preparation, but it is also a fact that when seeking to sell a business there can often be some scepticism on the part of the potential trade buyers, if it is presented on the basis that post sale, there will be more than the owner standing down from the company being acquired. This being acknowledged, moving Nick was, in effect, killing two birds with one stone: getting him off the SEL radar and providing DSI with a front man to get it on the road.

LIFE AFTER SYNSEAL

The magnitude of this concern with acquirers can vary depending upon the strategy of the acquiring company going forward. Sometimes, trade acquirers have their own existing management they intend to take over control of the business acquired. However, suspicions can also be aroused if too many senior members of the company being sold are seen to be short term employees, post sale.

Another time-honoured way of selling/buying a business is on an earn-out basis, which simply means that the seller will continue working with the business for a period of time after the company is under new ownership. This method has benchmarks of progress post sale, which provide for the seller to receive the agreed payment or balance payments, on attainment of certain criteria laid down in the sale and purchase agreement. I accept that on some occasions, there is little option than to enter into this type of arrangement, but personally, I don't like them. There is too much room for contention and skulduggery to take place. Notwithstanding the obvious financial issues, the concept of a guy who has been his own boss in his own business suddenly taking orders as an employee, is a recipe for problems. In line with my attitude to partnerships, I consider earn-outs to be a big No-No. The number of occasions when a company owner elects for an earn-out disposal as exit route, and subsequently bitterly regrets it, is rivalled only by the guys who go for a floatation, and find the city world with all its constraints equally distasteful.

Another situation where the existing staff is of paramount importance, post deal, is an MBO (Management Buyout). This is where the present management continue to run the company in an operational day to day fashion. In the case of such a deal, the company bought is usually acquired by a private equity company backed by debt providers.

Under such an arrangement, the existing staff are often incentivised by the acquirers, with nominal but potentially valuable share holdings. This type of process is usually referred to as a leveraged buyout. The seller is paid the agreed sum, and the investment company will put one or two people on the board of the company they have purchased. The intention is to grow or improve the business, until a point in the future when there is a further disposal. Then the P.E. company exits through a floatation on the stock markets or by way of a trade sale after owning the business for between 4 and 7 years. The arithmetic in these deals is fairly well-honed, and common amongst most of the P.E (Private Equity) Houses, as they are called. As a rough rule of thumb, the P.E. will be looking for an I.R.R (Internal Rate of Return) in the region of 20/30% across their portfolio of investments. This may seem excessive, but when one looks at the track record of such investment portfolios, it goes some way to explain the rationale behind such apparently ambitious expectations.

Although not very scientific, the saying goes that out of every three investments, one will bomb, one will wash its face, and the third will succeed. It is clear that in this scenario for every £100 invested in each of three acquisitions, the eventual return is not as excessive as it may initially appear. A simplistic explanation of a Private Equity House function is that it is normally a company with a mandate to secure money from outside sources, and use it's skills to invest these funds in a way that provides a good return for the original investors. As I have described, the risks to the original money providers are high, and they therefore demand a high rate of return. A P.E. company that invests well, and provides its investors/clients with a good return, is more likely to secure further money from the same clients in the future. In my view, there are only three basic categories of investment: cash, real investments (property for instance), and the markets in all its various forms and shapes: P.E, stock and shares, hedge funds, derivatives and too many more to mention. Always, it is a question of risk and return.

Having had my experience with the markets way back, when I dabbled with commodities, I know the markets are not to my taste. Maybe I am still the risk manager I aspire to be. I don't like the idea of some Tarquin taking a load of my hard earned cash and going out to invest/risk it on my behalf. I don't think I am a control freak, but I do prefer my destiny to remain as far as possible in my own hands.

Whilst on the subject of explanations, there is another point which deserves comment. 'Gearing' is one word interpreted differently in the business world. In my view, gearing is the word used to describe in percentage terms the amount of debt in a company, against the net worth of the company. Servicing of debt is simply the ability of the company to meet the repayments of debt.

'Leverage' is a word which means debt. A highly leveraged business is a business that holds a lot of debt on its balance sheet. Typical and simplified arithmetic of a leveraged buyout is, for instance, an M.B.O (Management Buyout), where the equity is held by the investors, the P.E. (Private Equity) Company and the management team. This cash investment will be calculated by the P.E. guys to provide the kind of I.R.R (Internal Rate of Return) I mentioned earlier.

Based on the prospects of the company in the future, and the purchase price negotiated with the seller, there will be a significant gap. That is usually taken care of in the form of 'senior debt', as it is described. The word 'senior' denotes the order of rank and priority of each money provider. The debt-providing banks will be charging a rate of interest at the outset which is commensurate with the markets at the time, but will be very much less than the P.E. and other equity holders seek to return. As such, the lower the return, the less risk they are prepared to take on. Therefore they get paid off before anyone else and the terms of the lending will reflect this. The whole concept of leveraged buyouts depends on the repayment of debt and the consequential increase in value of the equity.

I found a very simple way of understanding leverage. Say you buy a house for 100K, and put down a deposit of 10K, and borrow 90K. Then, after one year you sell it for 115K. After paying back the loan money, with an additional interest charge of, say, 5k, you return 20k for your original investment of 10K. The annual rate of return = 100%. This assumes there are no other costs involved, but you see the principle.

My plan was to seek a trade acquirer for Synseal, and I employed the services of a corporate finance advisor from one of the top four firms of accountants, KPMG. This chap called Morgan was to be responsible for the preparation of the company in all aspects, including sales information, memoranda, overseeing the due diligence document production, and the entire supervision of the presentation to potential acquirers.

Although I was certainly a more trained salesman, I most definitely needed the assistance, as this was a very specialised procedure. Morgan and I spent much time together, discussing the markets and possible candidates for buying the company. The strategy was to have everything in place to launch the sale to the trade buyer market during the back end of 2007 and start of 2008.

In a later chapter, I will summarise the reasons for a company offered for sale being regarded as good targets, and my rationale in examination and identification of businesses as good investments.

> **"VERY FEW WORDS WERE TABOO WITHIN THE SYNSEAL VOCABULARY, BUT UNIONS AND DOWN SIZING WERE TWO THAT WERE UNSPEAKABLE"**

BANG!! September 2007 – the crash started, and when others were trying to play it down, I somehow instinctively knew that this was not the usual home-grown recession, from which we could benefit, as in the past. This time it was to be different; not like previous recessions, which usually lasted between one and two years.

I called my team in, and explained my fears of the new world order that was appearing. I told the guys that I feared the situation would be long and difficult, and that we should prepare for the worst. Normally I would have expected to be berated by the team for such pessimism, but I think my passionate explanation and their own knowledge caused them to agree that we should tighten our belts regarding budgets, and look to weathering the storm, however long it lasted. If ever I had made a right decision, this was certainly one of those occasions.

I apologise for the continued use of the storm metaphor, but they do say that it is an ill wind that blows nobody any good. We needed to downsize, and part of this was a reduction in staffing levels, to most accurately reflect the reduced input of business. Never having enjoyed the prospect of making folks redundant, it was inevitable when looking to protect the beast that was the business.

The statutory redundancy selection process commenced, resulting in some 100 lay-offs. One of my failings in business is not having dispensed with people swiftly when it was necessary, but on this occasion there could be no prevarication. The situation was mollified when it coincided with part of the DSI (Door Stop International) preparation and the recruitment of staff. The upshot was the transfer of a number of personnel from SEL to DSI. These transfers not only mitigated the situation of SEL redundancies, but also provided the ideal opportunity to form an admin infrastructure at DSI. There were a number of seconds-in-command in the various departments at Synseal, who were capable and younger people, who had, to date, been assisting and understudying the directors and senior management. We were able to trim the SEL cost base, and produce a revised business plan, with commensurate revenue forecasts, to allow the continuance of the SEL sale process, whilst providing DSI with a staffing solution. With the benefit of hindsight, had I have known the seriousness of the economic debacle, I may have aborted or postponed the SEL sale. All the same, the governments of the world, the top financial experts, the banks and the accountants did not then realise the seriousness, so I don't beat myself up too much.

The search for a trade buyer for SEL was to continue. I don't have much of a reverse gear in my make-up.

Returning to DSI, Nick and I had a laugh about my plan to "send him next door" as first man out, on this occasion. Back in '95, when I sold the window division to JBS Industries, Nick was left as 'hostage' for three months until the new owners had a chance to get their own staffing properly in pace. That was 13 years ago, and Nick was no longer a kid, but had now developed into a capable businessman in his own right, so he was nominated as the man to go first.

I don't often like the modern parlance, but I do think that 'getting your ducks in a row' is appropriate to describe what we had embarked upon.

I was sharing my time between two primary activities: keeping up to speed with the progress of the DSI factory being set up, and the work involved with promoting the newly slimmed down SEL business for sale. Being ever the optimist, I convinced myself that the downturn could be used to advantage when presenting to possible acquirers. Buying a good company at this time would be a good investment when things returned to normal. This was to prove to be a bit of optimism too far.

Malcolm had his team perform in their usual manner and DSI was officially open for trading in April 2008. •

PLEASURE AND PROBLEMS

The year end for both Synseal and Door-Stop is March 31st, and the first quarter was devoted to the two main issues of DSI getting off to a flying start, and steadying the Synseal ship in choppy waters. There I go again, with my maritime metaphors!

At the same time, we began trawling through names of possible trade buyers for SEL.

Nick and the transferees from Synseal were ensconced, and I visited 'next door' on a regular basis. Malcolm and Steve Musgrave made frequent visits to maintain a watch on the production and other operational activities at DSI. By now SEL was referred to by DSI staff as 'Westminster', a nod towards the SEL size and status, no doubt.

Morgan, my corporate finance advisor, and I were collecting more potential candidates for presentations of the sale particulars. To this day, I wonder at the mind-set of the people involved in corporate finance, as they seem to have some sort of paranoia regarding letting the world and his dog know that a company is for sale. This flies in the face of my sales training, as I believe the more presentations you do, the better the chance of making a sale. They use strange expressions, one of which is kind of a code. When you see a report that a company is undergoing a 'strategic review', it often means it is up for offers.

I hold a similar view when I am asked by others if I drive my Rolls Royce and Ferrari to work. Some seem to think this is not good, because the staff will think that the boss is earning too much. I am diametrically opposed to this. My ethos is that if the boss looks as if he is doing well, then the company is regarded in a similar light; therefore the employees' jobs are secure. Many businessmen still don't regard security as an important issue to employees.

It is difficult for me to put into words the total hopelessness of trying to sell a serious company to the trade during 2008. Confidence was deteriorating by the day, banks were closed for lending, and a general atmosphere of fear and despair was permeating almost every corner of the commercial world. Previously active acquirers had gone to ground, and eventually the whole task of searching for a suitable buyer had to be abandoned in the autumn of that year. The cost of the due diligence report was significant, but I still felt that we would find it useable when we decided upon another tack in the attainment of the ultimate goal. There really is little else to say about this first stab at realising my exit ambitions.

Leaving aside the commercial side of life for a short while, there were a couple of things that happened this year that were enjoyable. Firstly, I decided to buy a larger boat with some of the giant dividend that I had paid myself. Carol, me and some of my crew spent time travelling to Italy, France and various other locations round the Mediterranean looking for our ideal vessel. I had been involved in the yachting world for 20 years by this time, and owned a dozen different craft. I have developed the profound belief that there are few proper business people connected to yachting at any level. In addition, with boats, it is always a question of compromise. If you get a bigger boat, then you have the extra comfort, space, facilities and sea-keeping qualities, but the downside is that it cannot berth in smaller ports, and of course it costs a damn sight more to run. Then there are extra crew, and no matter how selective an owner is when recruiting crew, there remains the fact that privacy is in some way diminished. I am a good ship skipper, and have gained much knowledge in all areas of the activity. I am not like most 'owners', as I see myself as a boat driver first and an owner second. I have done the time and learned the skills, and qualified to be a yacht captain. Knowing what boat I was looking for, it was simply a question of finding it.

During this time, I had the rather worrying situation in which my hair began falling out in ever increasing patches, all over my head. The idea of going bald was not one that filled me with glee, but it is not the end of the world for men to have no hair. I visited Bobby, my doctor, and he diagnosed alopecia. With some consolation, he told me that this would be temporary, and the hair would regrow in about a year's time. With some scepticism as to the accuracy of this prognosis, I decided that rather than looking like sort of piebald pony, I would shave the lot off, and did so in France. Looking different from the norm, I got used to it and so did others.

Doctor Bobby Ahmed was right: in about 9 months the hair started to return. The reason for the problem was the death of my brother. Since I experienced this occurrence I have explored the causes, and indeed it is not unusual for someone to suffer this type of reaction to such an emotional happening as losing someone close. It was two years after Stewart's death, and I was having a kind of post-traumatic stress reaction.

Dispensing with this not so pleasant occasion, I turn to the second pleasurable happening during 2008.

In May, I opened the mail at my home office, and was aghast to read the most beautifully composed letter from one Mr. Denis Brennan of the Cabinet Office.

I had been recommended to the Queen, to be considered for the award of an MBE (Member of the British Empire medal). I was elated and overwhelmed all at the same time.

Next... Some Business notes, spending £20M, setting on David Leng, getting the MBE and new boat •

INTERLUDE

Yacht Captain Gary, MBE – I did like the sound of this. DSI was moving ahead nicely and the new plan for my Synseal exit was soon to go live. But before we go there, I am intending that this chapter provides an interlude to the main story.

I will describe some further commercial convictions and lessons learned which some readers will find useful. I have used certain anecdotes to provide explanations for the origins of these beliefs.

If you don't feel the desire to indulge me by reading this part you will lose nothing of the story, just the business advice, so skip to the following chapter... The Boat Came In.

In no particular order:

- **The overtrading trap is very easy to be sucked into, either with your own or your customer's business. Things can be going well, and the thought occurs that it will not end.** *WRONG! This illusion of invulnerability is the slippery slope.*

Back in the '90s one of our biggest single customers was a firm with an owner who had much ambition, but limited ability. We will call him Jim. He was a very personable guy, as is often the case. Periodically, he would ask my advice, promise to do as I suggested, and then proceed to do the opposite. The upshot of this was that he opened more and more outlets, until it became obvious to me that he would ultimately run out of cash, and the ability to pay the £1/2M he owed for his SEL goods. I told him I would not continue supplying unless he provided a PG [Personal Guarantee].

His situation was a typical example of overtrading. Jim had what he considered to be a business model, and to an extent he was right. His method was to sell windows and doors which he manufactured from Synseal systems, and supply and fit to the householder. Jim's ever important lead generation was not too far from the Synseal method from years gone by. He opened a series of showrooms through the south of England.

There were two differences from when SEL followed a similar route. Firstly, it was 15 years later, and what worked then was not guaranteed to work now. Years ago, the market for buggy whips was considerably greater than it is today, if you see the crude analogy. The second and fatal mistake, was Jim not taking account of his cash resources and cash flows. Opening and launching new outlets gobbled money, and despite my warnings, he eventually ran out of cash and bingo! He was out of business. Jim had refused to give a personal guarantee, so I had ceased supply and he moved to a competitor. We got our money over 4 months and after a further 3 months he went bust, owing his new supplier hundreds of thousands of pounds.

- **Always instil in your colleagues an ethos to do as much as possible, not as little as they can get away with.**

- **Just because you have told a subordinate to do something, don't consider that you have been exonerated from responsibility when it does not happen.**
  People do what you inspect, not what you expect.

- **Remember, price is what people pay, value is what they receive. This is one of the all-time great statements in selling presentations.**

- **Try to avoid fighting the system.**
  When you have a VAT inspection, bear in mind that the guy attending is just a person getting a wage to do a job. 'Jobsworth' accusations are not recommended when in conversation with these people.

  Even if you are capable of showing off, and having all things in order, leave a little bit of corn for them to pick up. If they can find even the smallest item of 'discrepancy', they feel satisfied, and will often leave you to get on with making the money, from which you can pay the tax that pays their salary.

- When talking to a millionaire, don't expect the whole truth about how he made his first million. The explanation of how he obtained his latest million is likely to be more accurate.

- Economies of scale are often the route to super profits. This is one of the bedrocks of mergers and acquisition success.

- When someone complains that they need a bigger desk, be aware that it may result in a bigger mess.

- Customers always expect that you will do your job right in the first instance, but they don't expect you to put it right afterwards. Always regard after sales service as a marketing tool.

- Never be daunted by apparent authority. I have experienced policemen, soldiers and PLCs who think their status confers a right to be arrogant. The truth lies the other way: report a cop to his superintendent or a soldier to his C.O. or a PLC to the non-executive directors, and soon the arrogance will dissipate.

- Try to pick battles that you have a good chance of winning, or wait until you do.

- Try to remain true to the basic principles that served you well in the past.

- **Perfect the art of delegation.**

- **Never sacrifice vision on the altar of attention to detail OR the other way round.**

- **As you get on, don't get carried away with believing your own publicity.**

- **Try not to fall into the trap of attempting to turn a hobby into a business.**

  I have heard amateur flyers trying to justify their airplanes as being commercially viable. Golfers buy a golf course, nocturnal folks own night clubs. Trust me – if I ever had a business involving boats or shooting, it would fail. So long as you can keep an objective head with regard to your business, the better your chances of success. Thank goodness for plastic extrusion! No way could I become passionate about the product, only the business.

  One of the best radio interviews I can remember was when a guy who started a cheap flight business considered he had the Midas touch, and would be forever successful. The next interviewee was from a very successful career in TV. His view was that no matter how well you have done previously, there is no guarantee of repetition in the future.

- **Knowledge and experience do help the odds.**

- **Try to work within the confines of your own conscience.**

- **Think realistically but try to be positive. My glass is always half full, and never half empty.**

- **Remember Dr Peter's principle: "Employees are promoted up to level of their incompetence".**

- **Be aware of what industry (not sub-sector) you are in. Synseal for instance is in home improvements.**
  The old days of the American railways are good for demonstrating this point. Often these guys said they were in the railway business... Some said they were in transport and these were the ones who became leaders in air travel, coach travel and all things pertaining to transport.

- **If you come to recognise that one individual within the organisation is becoming indispensable, deal with it immediately, otherwise you will be in trouble.**

- **When buying existing businesses, I recommend as follows...**
  a. *Don't rely on VDD (Vendor Due Diligence). Do you own. More costly, but in my opinion essential*

b. *Always be aware that if a business is being offered for sale, there is going to be a degree of it being "Dressed for Sale".*

c. *Take a careful look at any closure costs which may be required. In the event of redundancies, employ experts to handle the process.*

d. *Don't be afraid to hive off parts of a newly acquired business, but again, make sure your advisors are top class. There can be a lot of unpleasantness resulting, from redundancies but be prepared to tolerate this for the greater good overall.*

e. *'Dumping the rump' following an acquisition can be an inevitable method of producing the best return on original investment. Basically, a restructuring and dispensing of some of the business acquired is sometimes preferable to soldiering on regardless. Again, this requires a specific skillset and should be undertaken with expert assistance only.*

f. *If dealing with publicly quoted companies, remember that these outfits are massively sensitive about publicity and can therefore be vulnerable to agreeing compromises which may work to your advantage.*

g. *Be very cautious when entering into No Publicity Agreements, they can prove very restrictive in future decision making.*

- **I have often been referred to as a margin buster. This I regard as a compliment, so long as margin busting does not include an unacceptable level of profit reduction.**

- **When someone asks for your help (or even advice), be aware they may not be asking for your opinion.**
  I have discovered that the person asking often wants you to confirm that they are doing everything correctly, and rather than what you consider to be constructive help, observation and criticism.

By way of a lighter note, and to finish this chapter, I am amused by the modern phraseology that has evolved over recent years:

THINKING OUT OF THE BOX...
We used to call this 'lateral thinking'

CHALLENGES...
We used to call these 'problems'

LOGISTICS...
Either 'operations' or 'distribution', or a combination of the two

HUMAN RESOURCES...
'Personnel'

ENGAGE...
'Dialogue' or simply 'talking'

Bloody political correctness! What a joke, if it were funny!

Let's move on! •

WHEN MY BOAT CAME IN, PART 1

Having bought our new yacht in the midst of the economic turmoil, there rose the question of bringing the boat back to my berth in France.

The preparations made before setting off on a maiden voyage with a new and unfamiliar vessel can be quite a lengthy process. The crew consisted of me; my co-captain, Rob; young engineer, Jez, and Mark, the chef.

Our passage plan was to leave Olbia in Sardinia and head nominally North, up the East coast to the Bonifacio Straits, and once having navigated through those, to move into open sea, on course for the Balearic Islands.

Anyone with any knowledge of geography will instantly realise that this is not the most direct route to the Côte d'Azur, France. The reason for this detour was to enable the boat to be TVA/VAT paid and registered within the E.U. (European Union). Spanish territory is the most cost effective area in which to facilitate this, and because we are talking several hundreds of thousands of Euros, then the trouble and extra time was well justified. Two or three percent in savings amounted to a chunk of money.

I have always been mystified by the massively differing rules and regulations over a huge range of issues throughout the E.U. I am more than an E.U. sceptic, and class myself as an E.U. detester. Just about everything about the E.U. is complete anathema to me. The duplicity, the corruption, the intrusion, the hypocrisy, the sanctimony of the majority of the morons working within the bureaucratic hell that the E.U. has become, is disgusting. And that's before we mention the lunacy of the concept of trying to integrate and assimilate all the differing cultures that make up this abomination. Thank God the UK stayed out of the Euro. Hopefully one day the whole thing will implode, and we can get away from this delusion of democracy, and return to sovereign states where each country is run by its elected representatives, not a heap of self-interested nobodies. I feel sure my blood pressure increases at the very thought of what damage Blair and then Brown perpetrated on our country. From illegal wars, to the sacrificing of our law-making powers, it is an obscenity. More tears and blood have been shed to keep Britain free, and now we appear to be handing over our independence on a plate, and paying for the privilege.

Meanwhile... back on the high seas, the first leg of our journey was anticipated in our passage plan to take some 20 hours, which of course would include night cruising. I decided to assert my right to take My Lady Rose (I like naming my boats after my granddaughters) from the port of departure for the first watch of 4 hours. Neither Rob nor I had previously helmed the vessel other than on sea trials, and this is very different from close quarter manoeuvring. I like to think that we are a team of professionals when it comes to the matter of actually handling boats. The crew and me are multi-tasking, and take our duties seriously. In addition, my personal experience of having spent a lot of years driving boats on inland waterways, as well as seafaring, has given me an above average

BEAUTIFUL TOY: MY LADY ROSE

ability when it comes to close quarter work. After slipping the lines in Olbia, it soon became clear that this beautiful Ferretti Yacht had a mind of its own when it came to responding to the commands from the bridge.

If you have ever wondered why boats are always referred to in the feminine gender; at the risk of sounding sexist, I have concluded that it is derived from the distinctly unique features that exist, differentiating one vessel from another. My Lady Rose has a hull shape that is not only attractive, but in some ways useful in certain sea situations. One of these features is not its quick response to the helm. I could rabbit on, but suffice to say, that I managed to exit the port without major difficulties and began to enjoy my new toy.

After several hours and watch/shift changes, I was again in the driving seat when navigating the Straits. These types of areas are notoriously choppy, and can be downright 'orrible when the winds are not conducive. We were now in the dark, and had a force 6 wind, which had picked up the sea to a state of three to four metres. For non-boating people, this means that even in a 180 ton, 31 metre vessel, the going can become very uncomfortable. When engaged in any passages longer than coastal daylight trips, there are always two crew on watch; when I was in command, Jez was there in the left hand seat. His job was to assist me in taking note of the array of instruments on the bridge, but mainly keeping a look out to sea. Night cruising on a calm sea can be very tranquil but remains potentially dangerous, as situations can quickly arise, which require a sure and trained response. Falling to sleep at the helm is unforgivable, but in fact it does happen more than most people realise. Therefore the understated job of the second guy on watch is to keep the helmsman fully alert; but with Jez I had more trouble keeping him from snoring.

Before I committed us to open sea for many hours, there was a point when I considered that the sea state was such that I might change course and proceed to a port of refuge down the west coast of Sardinia, to await the conditions improving. As we moved out of the Straits, the sea became less confused, and therefore I elected to proceed on our journey. The sight of land at daybreak is one that has always seemed quite surreal and inspirational. Even after one night, the sensation is both satisfying and romantic, but this might be a reaction more applicable to a Piscean achievement freak like me, than to other people.

The berthing in the Port of Mahon was fairly uneventful, and it was there, after a day of rest, that I was to call Net Jets and have the Citation Excel come and pick me up for a flight back to Blighty. The crew would need a couple of weeks to enable the Spanish authorities to take care of the taxing process, and it would allow them time to start all the myriad of jobs that constantly exist on boats, especially the larger and more complex type, which I now owned. With a new vessel familiarisation, and 'post shakedown' work to do, I am always happy to leave this to the crew. As I have learned in my business career, it is all about getting the right man for the right job.

I would return to Mahon after a while, and continue to share both the navigating and the experience of taking My Lady Rose into her new home, back in France.

Back home in the UK, there was work to do with the plan to sell Synseal, and to ensure Door-Stop International stayed on course.

Being a businessman is not too dissimilar to being a boat skipper: you have your plan, your crew/team, your objectives, and hopefully the necessary resources to get where you want to be. •

MEN
DOING
DEALS

WHEN MY BOAT CAME IN, PART 2

Following the miserable failure of the endeavour to sell Synseal to a trade buyer, my thoughts now turned to the alternatives, and the obvious of these was an MBO. The concept of a change of ownership of a company, transacted via an MBO process, is both simple and complex at the same time.

The management buying the business from the owner is understandable and rational. The management often believe that they have the requisite skills to take the business forward, and after a period of time, and a further exit process, they can perhaps make a capital gain themselves. Unfortunately, the ability to work in a business to help its performance and success does not necessarily equip people to take control of the company. My team at SEL was excellent, but were not really capable of taking over from me. And moreover, I suspect that there was not an individual who would have wished to take the job on.

Maybe Malcolm would have been the nearest candidate in terms of experience and knowledge of the company, and he had been the MD for a decade. However, Malc was not a consideration for a variety of reasons. His corporate knowledge was good, but not sophisticated enough to the level necessary to convince funders that he would make them the required return on their investment. His style of management, whilst effective, was unorthodox and unlikely to be perceived as the 'right' way. In any case, Malc would not have worked well with the semi-Tarquins, and nor would they with him. He would not want the position, and he was part of the 'Life after Synseal' plan, along with Nick and me. I had discussed the situation in considerable depth with Malcolm and Nick, and our intentions were well understood and co-owned. After my exit, I reciprocated the help Nick and Malc had provided me personally. In a pre-planned and programmed method, Nick had moved over to Door-Stop International, and at the appropriate time, Malcolm would follow.

Funders are understandably sceptical when making an investment, and one of their priorities is to maintain a committed team within any business they are funding. I was well aware of this particular issue, and I knew the strategy of getting the business away in poor economic times was going to be exacerbated in difficulty. This was because I was looking to sell without the continuances, the three individuals who had been integral to building SEL as market leader. I refer of course to Nicholas, Malcolm and myself. On top of this, I was intending to grow a new company in a similar market and with a product closely connected to Synseal's product range. SEL made doors, and DSI was going to be selling its products in the same market as Synseal. If I was to get the business away, it would be comparable to having swum the channel and climbed Everest simultaneously.

The tactic of taking both Nick and Malcolm off the Synseal team would be essential. It was again a question of timing, with a few added ingredients in the mix of objectives.

A little later, I was to make a move which hitherto had been an absolute no brainer for me. I would grant my two Generals share options. These would leave me in control, but would provide for a future sale of Door-Stop, in which Nick and Malc would each share in the proceeds. These options were crafted by the lawyers, so as to leave me with the discretion of parting company with the two men, without jeopardising my position. In reality, I would not look to replacing either of the two, but protection of my situation had become entrenched, so that's how it had to be.

With a deal the size of which SEL would represent, there was no way it could become a reality without the introduction of outside funding, and this meant having a very feasible and convincing business plan, with sufficient capable personnel to provide confidence in the minds of the investors. I needed to recruit a suitable person to lead the management team, and with a pedigree acceptable to the funders. This person was to be Mr David Leng. I had known David for several years, since he had at one time been the MD of a competitor company called Eurocel. During his time with Eurocel, he had demonstrated all the fundamental skills in the management of a reasonably large organisation, and throughout his career to date, had been involved in the various areas of acquisitions, disposals, restructuring, closures, and all things City orientated. After a preliminary exploratory conversation, David and I appeared to have what each other was looking for. He, in his late forties, was seeking an opportunity to have an equity share, to look to a capital sum coming his way a few years ahead. From my point of view, he was a credible person to present to the funders as the man to take the business and the team to new pastures.

When a business is taken over in the fashion of an MBO, and with all the leveraging incumbent upon such a deal, the investors clearly want the comfort that financial controls are of a high order. Brian Onions, my Finance Director for several years, had been involved in this type of scenario in his earlier career, but was more suited towards the trading company's fiscal management, in my view. He again was credible for the project and MBO. It is a fact that investors are often drawn towards a management team headed by a person from an accountancy background; I do not consider that accountants often make the best leaders. Without a doubt, their function is absolutely imperative to the wellbeing of any serious business, but when it comes to heading the enterprise, they can be a little too restricted in matters of vision, and sometimes cause the business to lose alacrity and flexibility.

By nature, accountants are people who can tear any proposed development to the bone, to a point where the idea seems nigh on impossible. I am a risk manager, but still acknowledge that risk is an unavoidable part of commerce.

There it was, David was on board at the end of 2008, and was intended to take over from Malcolm as MD, from the start of the next fiscal year, April 2009. The three months after his commencement was the time for David to familiarise himself with the company and its people. The guys were quite excited at the prospect of them having a small equity stake if the deal went through; they accepted David, and, I think, trusted my instinct.

During the first quarter of 2009, when David and I were preparing our plan for the MBO process, the appointment of a corporate finance advisor was at the top of this list of 'things to do'. David was working for me, but the eventual objectives were not mutually exclusive. I wanted out, and he wanted in – for the future. After having auditioned a number of candidates to work with us in the process, we appointed Catalyst Corporate Finance to the position of advisors. The function of advisors covers a wide area of duties, including seeking the interest of private equity companies, holding talks with debt providers, talking to solicitors and generally assisting with the presentation of the company on offer. Having already produced the Vendor Due Diligence document the previous year, when looking for a trade buyer, there were only a few amendments required to allow this information memorandum to be tailored to this new situation.

Synseal was a clean company, not having been dressed to sell. It was successful, and I believed that it could be attractive to acquiring investors on a 'what you see is what you get' basis. There had been no fancy fiscal massaging or engineering, but it was still a product for sale, and as such required the usual back to basics approach that had been my mantra for many years as a salesman. The polarisation of the industry had caused the future growth prospects of SEL to be envisaged in a largely 'buy and build format'. This simply meant that the company would best benefit from using Synseal as the vehicle and base for further acquisitions, in which the economies of scale and synergies would enhance the value for an eventual exit by the new shareholders. SEL had surplus capacity in most areas of its activity, including space, production, management and general infrastructure.

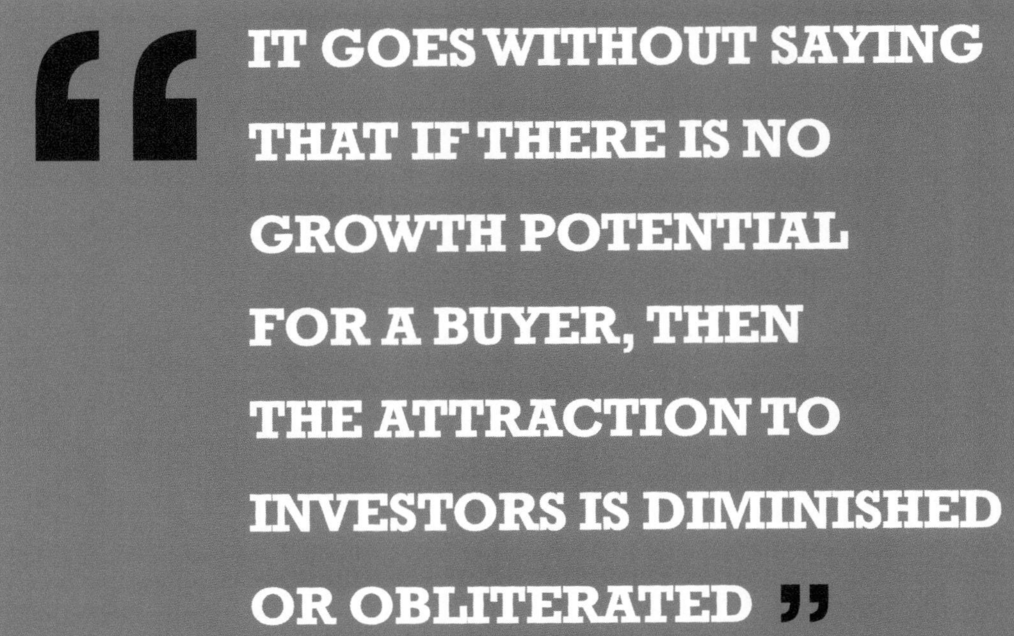

The world of company mergers and acquisitions is quite intense to the point where it has its own language. There is a lot of confidentiality, and the first example of this is the provision of a code name for the process. Ours was Project Dart.

Over the next year, we would be involved in a huge range of presentations and work covering environmental due diligence, commercial due diligence, contracts, legal restrictions, leasing of premises (which I was to retain and rent back to SEL), and much more. The widely used format for the sale is what is termed 'no debt, no cash', which means that if the company has borrowings, these would be deducted from any sale proceeds, and if the company had 'surplus' cash, this would be paid in addition to the purchase price. For determining the 'no cash' aspect, there are a couple of methods, either post completion accounts, or a locked box calculation. I had no intention of waiting until after the sale had taken place for my additional payment to be agreed, therefore the locked box was decided upon. In effect this entailed the parties agreeing the amount of cash that needed to be left in the company post sale to allow normal trading to continue, and the current assets adequate for this purpose. Any amount over and above this quantification went to the account of the vendor... me.

Back to the auditions, as I called them. David, me, and our man from Catalyst, Keith Pickering, held lengthy discussions with HIG Capital [Private Equity], culminating in arriving at heads of terms, in which HIG would be the major shareholders in the company after the completion of the sale. As I mentioned earlier, the role of the Private Equity Company is to invest an amount commensurate with their return ambitions and strategy. The balance of the monies over and above the P.E. tranche and the total price to be paid is made up of debt packages provided by the banks. Another strip of investment is through the management buying their shares, and occasionally by the vendor leaving some cash in, with a deal on interest paid over a period of time, and the capital repaid at a date in the future. In certain circumstances, it is necessary to include a strip of what is called mezzanine. This is used when a cash shortfall from the other mainline investors occurs, and whilst this can be very expensive, it can sometimes be the only way to prevent a deal-breaking situation.

As one would expect, the pecking order applied to the various fund providers is determined by a fundamental risk and return methodology. The banks who lend have the debentures over the company until their investment is repaid, and they hold the greatest authority over the company in respect of financing. In return, the debt providing banks are likely to receive an interest on their investment of something in the order of 5 to 7 %. The whole ethos of leveraged deals is to repay the debt as quickly as possible, resulting in the equity holders being in a position to achieve a far larger percentage return on their investment, which can be by way of floatation, resale or what is called a re-ratchet... a secondary MBO or MBI.

HIG and I had reached the point at which the price was agreed in principle, with the usual caveats and provisions for the investigating accountants to confirm that the state of the business was in line with the vendor's assertion. Paul Canning was the MD of HIG, the main man with whom I was dealing. Paul's associate was Andy Steel. Paul was a hard man in negotiations but it has to be noted that at the outset of any MBO all parties concerned have a common objective, in so much as, for differing reasons they all want the deal completed. They all have their individual motivation but still, they are in harness together. The vendor wants to sell for the agreed price, the management want to have a piece of the action and the P.E. house look for the opportunity to assist in growing the company in order to maximize their return on investment

My view on life, and one which I articulated frequently, was that I wanted the deal, but did not need the deal; this proved to be a way of keeping the P.E. guys from becoming too autocratic and greedy. In fairness the price agreed at the outset was eventually the price delivered. I believe this was in part due to HIG being an investor with integrity, plus I made it perfectly clear that I was not amenable to any moving of goal posts as the process progressed.

It has to be borne in mind, that the fees entailed in these types of deals can be enormous for accountants, solicitors, corporate finance advisors – and that's before the arrangement fees, charged by the other various lending institutions which become involved. As the process moves on, the fee clock ticks as well.

The single most difficult problem with this deal was the fact that the banks were, in a manner of speaking, closed for business. Whereas prior to the economic crash, banks had been prepared to provide debt calculated at anything between 5 and 6 times EBITDA (earnings before interest, tax, depreciation and amortisation), they were now either not prepared to back the deal at all, or were looking at 2 times EBITDA. It does not take a genius to recognise the impact this change had on the whole private equity backed acquisition world. The P.E. houses could not achieve a return sufficient to satisfy their investors if they were to put up the extra cash to facilitate a deal. Many M and As were aborted or postponed due to the extremely cautious attitude now displayed by the banks, which is a little irritating, when one considers that the whole situation was brought about by the banks' inept and greedy conduct.

The non-mutually exclusive objectives that prevailed were sorely tested, and I truly believe that the expertise and determination demonstrated by all concerned was the primary reason the deal eventually got across the finishing line.

Lloyds, HSBC, Barclays, RBS, Santander, Yorkshire and many more were all given the presentation and were all impressed with Synseal, but were either not inclined to make an offer or made a thoroughly hopeless, low proposal. Month after month, this performance continued, with David presenting the case for the management team, Paul Canning using his skills to procure the required senior debt funding, and so on. My part was to be available to speak with these institutions, and instil confidence in them that they would be backing a sure bet.

In order to make the arithmetic work for the P.E house, there was a requirement for an inclusion of about £30M of senior debt and it was anticipated at the outset that this would need at least two or more banks to provide the total. So much time was spent on these presentations that it became a complete nightmare. Some of the banks were swift to retreat from the negotiations, which was a blessing, but others dragged out their inevitable rejection announcements, creating not a little annoyance to us all. Heads of terms were agreed, and the date of completion of the sale was to be November 2009. One particular contender bank dropped out at the eleventh hour, leaving the closing date unachievable

I have always been conscious when involved in M and A activity, that the running of the company should remain a priority, and my team were doing their jobs, as ever. Paul, David and I were working hard together to find a solution to the debt package problem, and we remained stoical.

By way of an aside, MBOs have a unique aspect to them, which transpires as the situation progresses. At the outset, we are effectively all on the same track, but further down the process the individual players naturally become increasingly focused on their particular agendas. The expression used to describe this scenario in respect of the various advisors is that they go "native". Indeed I employed an additional corporate finance advisor to help with certain technical issues that arose.

MY NEW JOB AT DOOR-STOP

Having failed to complete the sale in November, the second deadline had passed, and I permitted further time for HIG to secure the essential senior debt packages. Now the last day of January 2010 was agreed as deal day.

I had made tax efficient arrangements for my CGT, which required me to commit to being responsible for paying over several millions of pounds in tax come the end of January. In effect if I did not meet this commitment, then the increase in CGT would be fairly horrendous. By the same rule, if I did pay it over to HMRC and the deal died, then it could be years before another sale opportunity arose, when I would be able take advantage of the tax preparations in place.

HIG were badly let down by another bank that had stated their intention to support the deal, only to drop out at the last minute. This was nothing at all to do with the quality of the deal, but rather the fact that when the bank's "committee" was asked to give final sanction, they ran for cover.

A few short years earlier and they would have been fighting to get in on the act. But this was now, not then.

On the same day that HIG asked for more time, leaving me with the dilemma of the tax position, my doctor, Bobby rang, and his words literally sent me to my knees. Carol had had some tests for chest pains and the results were that she had an acute case of angina. Bobby told me that she was to need surgery, and soon. Simultaneously, Carol was diagnosed as having a small lump in her breast, which would also need swift attention. What the fuck was happening? I was shattered and low, but knew I had no choice but to pull myself together and sort the problems.

Carol's father had suffered from angina, and I discovered from doctors that this illness is often hereditary, but this was no consolation to her or me. We chose not to inform her elderly mum, or anyone else for that matter. Whilst being sensitive to others, this only increased the pressure on us.

While I put conditions on the time extension HIG requested for completion, I had come to regard Paul as a very capable and genuine man. Although we were all exasperated with the current climate, we were minded not be beaten by the situation.

Improvisation in overcoming the senior debt providers' [banks'] faint heartedness was introduced, when HIG decided to provide what could be called a bridge. In effect they put in a very significant extra tranch of money, with the intention of this being "laid off" to the ususal debt providers at a later date. This initiative was the catalyst in enabling the completion to take place on the 23rd February 2010. I remain convinced that without the single mindedness and tolerance on the part of buyers and vendors the sale would have, as the expression goes, "fallen over".

The champagne tasted all the better for the joint commitment to completing a big deal in what I consider was the worst economic climate since WW11.

I conceived Synseal, gave birth to it and nurtured it to become a thirty year old adult. I retain a vested interest by way of ownership of the factories and some capital. However, I honestly say that I have the utmost desire to see the business develop and prosper because of my affection for the company and all who sail in her.

In an industry magazine some years earlier, I had been accused of having brass balls. Not a description I like; I was simply doing my job as best I could.

I do confess to having faced down the unions, and been very robust in various situations I experienced in business. We all have our own strengths and weaknesses, and my Achilles heel is most definitely wherever family is concerned. I had suffered alopecia after the terrible loss of my brother, and I was to have a similar but different reaction to the horrors of Carol being ill. It is for that reason, therefore, that I am not intending to elaborate on her several surgical operations, or the worst time of my life, walking round London on my own for 7 hours, before being overjoyed with the discovery that the doctors had succeeded, and my wife was to be OK. After three months, Carol had recovered, and is now as good as ever.

The only testaments I would like to make, are firstly to the unbelievable bravery my wife demonstrated, and then secondly to the fantastic work of the surgeons, Mr Kamran Baig, Mr Douglas Macmillan, and Mr Carlo Di Mario. To all of them, goes my undying gratitude and admiration. I will tell shortly of the way in which I choose to try and reciprocate the work of these great men. As regards Carol's illness, it is too emotional to go into further.

Deal Day Cometh, 23rd February 2010.

On the 23 rd of February at approximately 6.35 pm and along with much popping of corks, the sale was completed. It is always an interesting and exciting time; all the people concerned, having spent months negotiating, suddenly become relieved and congratulate each other. This occasion was no exception; we had conference calls open between the solicitors and other representatives involved. Once the monies had been confirmed as correct and transfers confirmed by the lawyers that was a "done deal"

One aspect that made this time particularly funny was that the conference calls had included people in the Isle Of Man, Miami, London, various parts of Europe and my HQ in the less glamorous Huthwaite Notts.

I do consider that there are many a parallels between the game of chess, the military and business.

Perhaps worthy of a mention is the influence the 2008 crash, and the banking situation, on my attitude change. From being a "cash is king" sort of a guy hitherto, there transpired a fear of banks going bust and taking my money with them. The upshot of this was the some what rapid spending of about £20m. Ok, I was intending to buy the new boat and the DSI factory, and for sure I had a great big tax bill to pay but with my increasing paranoia I elected to complete all three of these transactions in a matter of 4 days. Amazing, the feeling of relief at having reduced the overall cash resources of the company and me by £20m. My tax advisor told me that I was not alone in the transfer of cash for more tangible assets. •

THE NEXT CHAPTER

Door-Stop International was designed as a lifestyle business, which is a sort of metaphor for a low stress company that pays the principals salaries that are not really appropriate to the effort. But then again, as I always preached, I pay for results, not effort.

My role is that of a cross between a non-exec chairman and the executive variety. Nick is MD, and Malc, CEO. Their actual functions did not change too much from the SEL days. Nick focused on getting the business in, and Malc's, along with Big Rob's, Mathew's and Jacky's roles, were to get the operation running like a machine, and ensure the product quality was high, with the service to match. Delma, my long time secretary, had moved from Synseal, along with several others including Mark Robinson, the finance manager.

I told the guys at the outset that I would not be as operational, day to day, as was the case in the past. I maintain my responsibility to keep overall credit control, and my Chairman's duties, along with the general strategic planning, and usual assistance with the marketing and other areas. This activity takes the form of informal brainstorming sessions, often over a bottle of wine in my office late in the afternoon.

After a few teething problems had been dealt with, and after my joining, the business has gone from strength to strength, which in reality it should do. We had all the resources, a great new product, plenty of experience, and the 5 million loan capital which I injected to get the show on the road.

We also had our not so secret weapon, the ultra-important UPS (Unique Selling Point), which on this occasion was our 'three days from order to delivery' service. The original marketing policy revolved around this exceptional feature.

As ever, we ran on a commercial basis, with me charging market rent for the factory I owned, and charging DSI interest on the loan at 5% over LIBOR (London Inter-Bank Offer Rate).

We had good staff, a quality product, excellent service and prices producing good margins, and we have little serious competition. We were, as ever, focused on our sales and marketing to a high degree. I have conjectured that the reasons we have seen no competition of any consequence are the cost of entry, the unbeatable USP, and perhaps the reputation we gleaned at Synseal, as being mega aggressive when challenged in the market place.

My time now is split between DSI and researching investment opportunities, which are to be my way of ensuring that my other product, money, produces a suitable return. Being the risk manager, and having a healthy contempt for the City, and all that goes with it, my resolution was to leave the structured products well alone, and buy investment properties, primarily in the £2-5 million bracket, with good tenants and covenants, with decent lease terms for as long a period as was available.

Thinking back to the structured products so loved by the City types, I recall having been involved in several of the species over the years. There was my foray into the options market, the platinum sponge NI avoidance scheme, the profit related pay for staff, the mortgage hedge deal, the Isle of Man CGT avoidance method, and last but not least the SSAS pension for which the government have since moved the goal posts. In every single case I can honestly say that I have regretted - with varying degrees of magnitude - ever becoming involved. I regard them all as rubbish for all concerned, except the firms with which I arranged these abominations.

The other area, which was to become very important to me, was the matter of reciprocating support for the people who had been so very good in helping my wife to recover from her illnesses. I knew I was never going to become a medical person, and the prospect of becoming involved with politics, which had been offered to me on several occasions, was rejected on the basis that I don't respond well to committees, and the plethora of idiots that seem to infest many political environments.

The choices being narrowed down, the answer was to use my money to show my gratitude for the help Carol had received. I was not minded to be too general with my contributions, so I had several meetings with the actual doctors and surgeons, who had been involved with my wife's illnesses. I set up two philanthropic activities: The Dutton Endowment for Clinical Academic Cardiology, and The Dutton Oncoplastic Research Fellowship. Including gift aid, these two causes received £250,000 each. I may well contribute more money in the future. In fact, all royalties that this book may generate for me will go directly to these good causes.

I am resolved not to contribute to anything other than medical causes. Music and sports are ok, but by no means as important as I regard medicine to be. The idea of backing a fourteen year old girl with a talent for tennis, only to find that at sixteen she has discovered boys and vodka, does not motivate me to pull out my cheque book. From my involvement with the Nottingham University side of my philanthropic work, I have been asked to give talks on my specialist subject of building businesses to students taking degree courses in business. I enjoy these, and have committed to making myself available for others in the future.

It is quite a new experience for me to work for no pay, but maybe as they say: you get on, you get honest, and then you get honourable.

On the matter of honours, I was invited to become a member of the University College of Benefactors last year. The college is very exclusive, and the induction ceremony very inspirational, although I did perhaps feel a little ill at ease being presented in my robes and mortar board headgear, but still another memorable occasion.

Alongside my charitable works, and using my way of finding a man to assist me, I have become reasonably knowledgeable in the commercial property investment field, having decided that this is where my investment strategy will be targeted. That said, if an opportunity to become involved in another trading enterprise presented itself, I may not be able to resist.

That is not far from the end of my story to date, and I do truly hope that it has been of some interest, and maybe a little help in providing food for thought, for people taking their place in the business world. The journey for me has not always been a bed of roses, but has provided me with so many things, in so many different ways. It would be disingenuous

DRESSED FOR THE OCCASION, MY INDUCTION TO THE COLLEGE OF BENEFACTORS NOTTINGHAM UNIVERSITY

for me to say that the material side is anything but great, but similarly, and in a more soulful sense, the convictions, philosophies and knowledge I have acquired have provided considerable satisfaction.

In the final summary, I give a few more examples of these. If you have had enough, I don't mind if you close the book now.

I never set out to write a rags to riches tale, but from my modest beginnings with no O levels, to being named in the Rich List, and with my boat Captain's licence, MBE, being acknowledged by academics and other alumni, and now with the title of author, I do feel that the journey has been worth the trouble.

Good luck! •

A FEW FOR THE ROAD

1. There are two basic types of entrepreneurs, those that find a product for a market and those that find a market for a product. I have always been of the second variety. I don't get original ideas but can turn a seed into a forest. Decide which category you fall into.

2. A good acid test for me has always been "Would I buy this product?" If the answer is no, and for the correct reasons, you may find others don't want it either.

3. Remember that just about everything that happens in a business can be used in the marketing department. If your receptionist takes too long in answering the telephone, this does nothing to create good P.R. Your company letterheads can give a good or bad image, and so on.

4. Zero to hero is great, but rarely occurs. Real success invariably takes a while, Mark Zuckerberg of Facebook excepted.

5. There is no point bribing or threatening someone to run a four minute mile if he can't do it. Put square pegs in square holes, or get someone who can perform as you require.

6. We all know the text book definition of economics, consumption, social science, etc. I have considered that the simplest way to understand the rudimentary meaning of the words 'market economy' is to think supply and demand, coupled with what people want, not what they need.

7. If ever dealing with private equity companies, or a business trade buyer for that matter, be aware that no matter how much due diligence is carried out, there will remain a view that post deal there will be some skeletons or black holes in the business purchased. I found it important to make clear the fact that I did not need to sell the company, but did indeed want to sell it. I use the expression that goes "Businessmen get on, then they get honest, and then they can afford to get honourable." Three months after selling Synseal in 2010, I was asked "Is there anything you can tell me that you did not want to come out during the negotiations?"

8. Always be ready when selling a business to answer the question "What's the worst thing that could happen to this business?" It is good practice to know the answer when you are at the helm. Without this knowledge you may well be caught out by insurmountable circumstances. With Synseal it was a catastrophic tool breakdown. It took 6 months to obtain a replacement, and no amount of money would materially reduce this time lag. We always kept back-up tools, which was expensive, but otherwise it was potentially fatal.

9. Exporting is totally different to doing business in your own country, and requires a lot of different skillsets in order to facilitate success.

10. I believe that the real drivers of the economy are often the average Mr and Mrs. Sadly the politicians seem to ignore this quite frequently.

11. When you are the boss in your own business, you must realise that you are the mortar between the bricks, and must focus on strategic decision making and attention to detail, simultaneously.

12. Never be intimidated by a bigger and apparently more impressive organisation. They are, in my experience, too far from "the street", and become vulnerable to a "sucker punch" if you stay alert.

13. Don't try to buck the markets. In September 1992 our Chancellor of the Exchequer, Norman Lamont, tried and failed, when he attempted to keep the value of the pound sterling up by buying the pound. Nonetheless, interest rates went from 10% to 12% to 15% and back down again in a matter of hours. The markets still sold the pound, and the exchange rate for the pound fell, as we were out of the ERM (Exchange Rate Mechanism). Personally I view the Euro and the E.U. as unsustainable. The concept of having a common currency is OK for Germany to export its goods without the challenge of its client countries devaluing their currency, but it is, as I write, coming back to bite them. The common market was a good idea I believe, but it has become adulterated. What price democracy when we have our sovereign state dictated to by some half-wit, non-elected, gravy train self-important bureaucrats in mainland Europe.

14. If you are looking to buy/merge a business, what are the basics to look for? Ensure the company targeted is still cum growth, otherwise discount the price accordingly. Look for synergies and economies of scale with your existing enterprise(s). Look at the reasons the vendor is seeking to step down. Some of these I list:

a. No team to improve or run the business as it is or as it grows

b. No dynasty

c. Ill health

d. Marital problems. Many a time a person has to sell in order to realise cash to settle a divorce

e. Wants to extract cash or cannot acquire more funding to maintain/grow the business

f. Simply the owner is too old or the business is now too big for him

g. Bad housekeeping, Often there can be a decent gross margin but little or no net. The cost base and overheads can be out of control and sometimes this can be rectified with reasonable ease

h. The owner may simply have desire to do other things with his life and time

i. Getting rid of a competitor is a very good reason to consider an acquisition particularly if your medium/long term strategy is to grow to a critical mass state more quickly and then exit yourself

There are many, many more points to be aware of but these give you a flavour for what to look for.

Terminology can be something of a minefield. When negotiating, ensure you have the same understanding of trading profit and operating profit. Other areas where this is prevalent is the gearing definition, and cash positive/ cash generative.

Occasionally sit down and list the ways in which you can grow your business. This may seem obvious but you can sometime miss the obvious i.e.

a. Sell more for less
b. Sell less for more
c. Sell the same for the same but cut costs (I prefer the expression improve efficiencies)
d. Look at added value possibilities
e. Integration either vertically or horizontally
f. Franchise (not my way, but many have done okay with this e.g. McDonald's)
g. Acquisition/ mergers.

15. Try to remember that the concept of living in a world of freedom of speech is largely an illusion. In the commercial world, as well as our lives in general, we are increasingly subject to penalties for stating an opinion - truthful or not.

16. If you become successful, don't start to believe your own publicity. The idea of having the Midas touch can prove very expensive. Not only is the repetition of success not guaranteed, but there is another area of vulnerability. People who have accumulated wealth in their business careers will sometimes become bored following an exit or partial exit from their previously busy commercial lives. A situation can result whereby a young, inspirational person can be very convincing and plausible when describing to an "Old Hand" a new and exciting venture. When the successful person becomes involved for reasons of ego, vanity or simple boredom it can sometimes prove to be the road to serious reduction in previously hard earned wealth.

17. When asked to adjudicate a contentious issue concerning a commercial situation, always ensure that you listen carefully to the evidence for the prosecution as well as the defence...or the other way round.

18. Rightly or wrongly, I have resolved that a degree of cynicism will develop in a successful person's mentality in general. With me, this has

taken the form of largely regarding commercial adversaries as guilty until they prove themselves innocent.

19. I make no claims to being a takeover expert, but this was never my main claim to fame. However, of course I have developed certain views in respect of calculating price of businesses for sale. One of these is to compare the price being asked against [where practical] a "green field" start up.

This is a very rough and ready method and really only reinforces my point made earlier that you must get the right man for each job. Employing top class corporate finance advisors, solicitors, accountants and last but by no means least, tax experts, is essential. Put square pegs in square holes

20. One very final point. We have all heard the expression: "I don't want to be a millionaire, I just want to live like one". If anyone has actually performed this feat, I would be interested to hear how it is achieved? •

POSTSCRIPT

I look forward to the future with some trepidation, in the sense of the family getting older, but more especially, the ever-changing way of the world. So many things have changed for the better, and will continue to do so, I have no doubt. However, as with most things, there is a downside. We must accept that globalisation will erode the English way and the sovereignty that has existed for centuries.

In some ways, perhaps, we will benefit from the extinction of the pomposity, arrogance and establishment which I believe have defined Britain for too long. Unfortunately, I fear this will bring with it an ethos of wishy-washy liberalism that will serve no purpose, save for the self-serving minority, who see such evolution as their opportunity to clone us further. I hope, with profound pessimism, that we will retain a majority of people who are caring and have a social conscience, whilst understanding the consummate reality that people are, and will forever remain, individuals.

Long live the Kingdom, real democracy and the right for everyone to strive to better themselves for the good of themselves, their family and friends, and ultimately, I believe, for the good of the country. •

A

B

C

D

E

F

G

H

I

J

L

M

N

O

P

R

S

T

U

V

W

Y

AMAZING
AUTHORS

CPSIA information can be obtained
at www.ICGtesting.com
Printed in the USA
LVIW021250140512
2824LVUK00003B